BROKEN LINKS

RESTORING OUR CONNECTION TO GOD

ANTHONY CARAVETTA

Story **BUILDERS** P R E S S

Published by StoryBuilders Press

Paperback: 979-8-89833-039-2

Hardcover: 979-8-89833-040-8

eBook: 979-8-89833-041-5

To my wife, whose love and support inspire me to be a better man, and to my children, who challenge me to grow as a husband, father, and follower of Christ. You are my greatest blessings and my reason for striving to live with purpose and passion every day.

Contents

Dear Reader,

If you're holding this book, there is a good chance you're searching for something—clarity, peace, purpose, or simply a deeper closeness with God. I want you to know this from the beginning: You are not alone.

Over the years, I've met so many people—brand-new believers, lifelong faithful churchgoers, pastors, parents, young professionals, retirees—who quietly confess the same struggle:

"I believe in God…but something still feels missing."

We expect our faith to make life feel easier, calmer, more fulfilling. But in reality, we often feel stressed, overwhelmed, disappointed, or spiritually dry. We wonder what's wrong with us, or worse, we assume God is silent.

I wrote Broken Links because I've lived those moments too.

And through prayer, Scripture, and personal experience, I discovered a truth that changed everything:

Our salvation is secure, but our daily connection with God can still break or seem distant.

Not permanently, not irreparably, but subtly—through our habits, our distractions, our fears, and our worldly patterns. And once those "links" weaken, we lose touch with the peace, strength, and direction God longs to give us.

This book is my attempt to help you rebuild that connection, not through formulas or spiritual pressure, but through an honest, practical journey back to the heart of God.

My prayer is that these pages remind you of who God is, how deeply He loves you, and how close He truly is, even when you don't feel it.

I pray that as you read, the broken links begin to mend.

With grace and gratitude,
Anthony

Introduction

*To be controlled by human nature results in
death; to be controlled by the Spirit results in
life and peace. Those who obey their human
nature cannot please God.*

(Romans 8:6, 8 GNT)

When you die, what will happen to you?

Can you be sure?

There's an old joke about four friends who die and find themselves at the Pearly Gates. St. Peter is there, checking on them before they enter. St. Peter says to them, "Come. Please look here below. You can see and hear your family at your funeral. What would you like them to say about you as they say goodbye?"

The first three all say pretty much the same thing: "I'd like my family and friends to say, 'He was such a good man—God-loving, respectful, honorable, a hard worker for his family. He led by example.'"

When it's the last friend's turn, he is still looking confused and wondering how he got there. St. Peter again asks him, "Please, my son. What would you like your family to say at this moment?"

The friend looks around, looks down, sees his family standing around his casket, looks back at St. Peter, and says, "Well, honestly, I'd like everyone to say, 'Wait a minute! Look! He's moving! He's not dead!'"

It's a funny story but also one that carries a grain of truth. If we're honest, most of us are not ready to die. How many of us right now on earth would be comfortable meeting God—our Maker and the Creator of the universe—to give an account of our lives?

If you asked most people whether they want to go to heaven when they die, they would likely say yes. In fact, the majority of Americans believe they're on their way to heaven. A much smaller number believe they're headed to hell. According to author and teacher Randy Alcorn, a survey found that more than 120 people believe they're going to heaven for every one person who believes they're going to hell.[1]

Others are simply unsure. Maybe you're one of them.

Most people know their lives have had a lot of ups and downs. As we get older, many of us recognize that we haven't always been good or kind, and we haven't always done the right things. We know we've been selfish and self-serving. We may *wish* and *hope* we'll "get into" heaven, but many of us just don't know for sure or lack conviction that we will.

If that's how you feel, you may be struggling with despair and a lack of hope, direction, passion, meaning, significance, and purpose. You may feel like you're limping through life, dragging one leg behind you. And you're not alone. Even some of the most pious people struggle, feeling the weight of life's difficulties and their circumstances.

There are many who don't want to think about the fact that someday we will die, our bodies will deteriorate, and our souls will enter eternity. Still others don't believe in eternity or the afterlife at all. But if heaven and hell are real and going to one of them is a certainty, wouldn't you want to know where your soul is going for all of eternity?

The Problem: Our Broken Relationship with God

God created us—all of humanity—to love Him with our hearts, souls, minds, and strength, and to love our neighbors as ourselves (Mark 12:30–31). We were made to live in perfect relationships with God and each other. God made us with an internal alarm, or conscience, to filter what is right and true from what is wrong and false.

The problem is that we sinned and broke our relationship with God. We are lost and unable to find our way back onto God's chosen path for us. Our alarm is still there to alert us when questions pop up in our hearts and minds, and we wonder if we're doing the right thing. Usually, the answer is clear. Our internal, God-given alarm sounds, reminding us to examine our thoughts, actions, and behavior.

Sadly, we often find it easy to ignore what our conscience is telling us. We tell ourselves that what we want is more important than what God wants. Just as a lying, cheating husband can't have a meaningful, true, deep, intimate connection with his wife, the same is true of our relationship with God. Our wrong behavior separates us from a close personal relationship with God.

We let our sins come between us and God. Our connection to God weakens when we keep on sinning and living for ourselves without consideration for those around us. Sometimes we may turn to Him for help or ask for a miracle. We may even ask for a sign or an answer. But because we're so disconnected from Him due to our own actions, we find it extremely difficult to hear His voice.

We often let the busyness and worry of our lives get in the way of our connection with God. Most of us spend our time worrying and trying to control situations and circumstances within our families, work environments, local communities, neighborhoods, and churches. It's absolutely exhausting. Doesn't it make you tired just thinking about it?

How can we have a relationship with anyone—spouse, child, parent, sibling, coworker—if we only talk to them once every few weeks or months, only on holidays, or when we need something? That's not a healthy relationship.

Times like these lead us to wonder where God is when something really bad happens. And when we can't hear Him, we ultimately blame Him for the things that go wrong. This is not how our relationship with God should be. He is more than a get-out-of-jail-free card or a genie ready to fulfill our wishes.

At some point in our lives, we finally start realizing that we can't control the world around us. We can't keep life from being hard. Should we just give up and say, "That's life"?

Or is there a better answer?

The Solution: Strengthening Our Connection with God

Every person has a hole in their heart that only God the Father can fill and make whole. That hole is what we are always seeking to repair. Even though many of us have had difficult parents, we must realize that our earthly fathers can't possibly meet our needs and provide the supernatural healing power that only our heavenly Father can give. Without God, we will spend our entire lives seeking to fill the void that only He can fill.

Thinking of God as a father may be difficult for some. It's hard not to project our relationships with our parents onto our expectations of God. If we had a good relationship with our parents—supportive, loving, caring—we likely see God in the same light. However, if we grew up without a father's presence, we may feel like God will abandon us someday. If our dads were volatile or physically and verbally abusive, we will probably have difficulty trusting God. If our fathers were unreliable, unpredictable, inconsistent, or hard to please, we may struggle to believe God is all-loving, unchanging, and dependable.

The Bible tells us that God is the same, yesterday, today, and forever (Hebrews 13:8). Our earthly fathers were sinners just like we are. Their connection with God may have been lost years ago, and they may have struggled just to get through life. God is not like our earthly fathers. Our minds can't comprehend how much He loves us. *Trying to understand God's power and love for us would be the equivalent of a person trying to explain the Internet to an ant.*

The only way to fix our relationship with God is to trust Him, turn to Him, and confess our deepest thoughts, feelings, desires, and faults to Him. When we confess our sins to God, He washes them away. God's Spirit comes over us, and our connection to God the Father is restored.

From that point on, your connection with God is what you make of it. If it's important to you and you want to spend all of eternity in heaven, you will make your relationship with God a priority. As you seek Him, you'll see Him in many things around you. You'll speak, think, and reach out to Him often with praise, gratitude, love, and requests for help. Like a young child who loves his parents, we will be drawn to act and think about God all the time.

Pastor Rick Warren said, "You can't always control your circumstances, and you definitely can't always control the way you feel. But you can control what you think about. That's *always* your choice."[2] Even though we will never be able to control everything that happens to us and around us, we can take full control of our attitudes, perspective, and outlook.

Stop Trying to Control the Uncontrollable and Start Working to Control Your Mind

Since we can't control our circumstances or the situations around us, why do we continually try to control the uncontrollable? The Bible encourages us to "take every thought captive" (2

Corinthians 10:5 ESV) and to "be transformed by the renewal of your mind" (Romans 12:2 ESV).

Our minds are more than just our brains. Our minds are our thinking, understanding, reasoning, perspective, and attitude. Once we start taking control of our minds, we can change how we view the world and how we treat those around us. And we can strengthen our connection with God, our Father.

God is always in control. He is sovereign, the initiator and sustainer of our relationship. Everything we do is because God started everything for us. From birth, our first breath, our food, clothing, warmth, safety, protection, resources, health, jobs, and so on—He gave us all those things. In response, we try to give back our time, talents, and treasures.

The very reason we pray and seek God is that He spoke to us first. We can know what He's saying to us now by reading the Bible. Prayer starts with listening to God. We first read His Word, study it, digest it, and write it on our hearts. By doing so, God speaks to us, and we listen. Just as in any good relationship, the more you listen and pay attention to the one speaking, the more you grow toward and with that person.

As the Old Testament prophet Daniel wrote, "I turned my face to the Lord God, seeking him" (Daniel 9:3 ESV). By turning our face toward God, we'll hear Him speak to us. We'll understand His plan for us, His purpose for us. We'll realize that He's a good God who loves and helps us. He knows what's best for us, and He gives us what we need. However, that always happens in God's perfect timing, which isn't always ours.

Although God initiates and sustains our relationship with Him, relationships are not one-sided. We have the responsibility to pray, seek, and ask Him for our heart's desire. These are our responses to His grace, mercy, love, and forgiveness.

Are We Really Forgiven?

Forgiveness is a hard concept, isn't it? There have been plenty of times when I hurt family members, friends, girlfriends, teammates, classmates, and even strangers. Most of the time, I felt sorry afterward and tried to apologize and seek their forgiveness. But I often still felt the guilt and shame of my actions. I still felt like I wasn't worthy of forgiveness. I felt like the relationship was tainted because of my words or actions—that our connection could never be the same.

Have you ever hurt someone so deeply that you were afraid you would never be able to repair your connection with them? Or maybe someone has hurt you in that way.

Repairing a relationship that has been broken can be extremely difficult. Even if the hurt person actually truly forgives the other, the offender still struggles to fully accept the hurt person's forgiveness. That is why the relationship can't heal, why they don't feel as close, and why the connection isn't restored.

I believe this happens with our connection to God as well. When we go through bad circumstances, pains and struggles, sickness and death, trials and tribulations, we sometimes blame God, curse others around us, and strain our connection with God for some time. Even when we repent and ask Him for forgiveness, we still struggle to feel connected to Him.

We have to remember that God never leaves us. He tells us there isn't anything we can do or not do for Him to make Him love us any less or any more than He already does. Sometimes we try to leave God and turn away from Him. Sometimes God allows these things to happen so we will turn back to Him and seek a stronger relationship with Him after we've experienced the pain that comes from being without Him.

Think about all the parents of college students around the country during peak COVID times when their children were sent home for remote learning. Who do you think was happier—the parents or their children? Most loving parents welcomed their children back home with open arms and rejoiced to have them under their roofs again during those times.

How much more will God embrace us and welcome us home each time we come knocking at His door. Like our earthly parents, our heavenly Father wants us back home under His roof. God is the creator of everything and everyone. Because we have a restored relationship with Him through the work of His Spirit, we are part of God's family.

God, who is always predictable, never changing, and never moody, will always want the strongest and most impactful relationship with us, unlike our worldly relationships that change from day to day. Too often we put our trust in our homes, family members, friends, jobs, and finances, but all these things can and will let us down. But God *never* changes (Malachi 3:6). He's always constant and consistent for all of eternity. He always keeps His promises (2 Corinthians 1:19–20).

When our connection with God feels broken, it's because of our own actions. God is always there waiting for us. He wants the strongest relationship with us—a fortified, unbreakable bond. We're the ones who weaken the bond and fall away from Him at times. That's why we constantly need to turn to Him for salvation like our lives depend on it—because our lives *do* depend on it.

Are your heart, mind, soul, and strength heading toward God and His values and character?

How can you know for sure?

Living by the Flesh or Living by the Spirit

The greatest commandment is this: "Love the Lord your God with all your heart and with all your soul and with all your mind and with all your strength" (Mark 12:30). But how is it possible for us to do that? God created us to love Him in all those ways, so He equipped us with that capacity. Until it was interrupted by sin, it was our natural inclination.

Our words usually reveal what's in our hearts. We can love God with our words, being quick to listen and slow to speak, choosing to build up others versus tearing them down. We can choose to use our words for encouragement and inspiration.

Loving God with our soul comes from our feelings and attitudes that are rooted in our perspective. A thoughtful, grateful soul allows us to love God by showing compassion to others.

When we are considerate and graceful toward others, we're loving God with our minds. And we can have loving, humble, gracious attitudes and perspectives.

And finally, we can love God with our strength through doing, through our actions, and by making a lasting contribution to our family, friends, church, and community, which impacts the world. Being a servant leader and giving back to our churches, neighborhoods, and communities reflect loving God with our strength.

We serve God not out of duty or obligation but out of love, grace, and gratitude with a meek and humble heart. Those make our connection with God strong. God gives us faith and love as gifts. As we see throughout the Bible, faith grows the more we use it and put it into action.

The Bible tells us how to know what weakens and what strengthens our connection with God. The book of Galatians calls behaviors and actions that harm our relationship with God "walking by the flesh." They include hate, jealousy, anger, selfishness, sexual immorality, envy, drunkenness, and worshiping anything other than God (Galatians 5:19–21).

The opposite set of behaviors and actions, the ones that make our relationship with God stronger, are called "the fruit of the Spirit." They include love, joy, peace, patience, kindness, goodness, faithfulness, gentleness, and self-control (Galatians 5:22–23).

How can you know if you're going to heaven?

Consider which path you're on now. One path leads to restored relationships with God and others, and ultimately to heaven. The other doesn't.

My hope is that this book will push you to examine your life's trajectory—where you are heading—and help you determine where you want to be. If you're going in the wrong direction, you will not end up at your hoped-for destination. If you're turned away from God and keep walking away from Him, it will be extremely difficult to meet God and stay connected with Him as time goes on.

In the next chapters, we will look at the ways walking by the flesh weakens and breaks our connection with God. We'll also discuss how we can mend and strengthen our relationship with Him.

But first, I want to share with you a vision I had of the links that connect us to God.

Broken Links

A few years ago, I had a vision that impacted me so greatly that I immediately had to write it down. I saw an image of God's mighty hand holding onto a massive, unbreakable, solid ring. Beneath God's ring were several others of various sizes and thicknesses, forming a chain reaching down from heaven. The last link, the one I could grab onto, looked similar to God's, but it was much smaller and thinner.

This vision has been with me every day since then and is now part of my prayer process. I've shared it with friends and family, and even my children have been thinking about it and attempting to draw the image themselves. I'm not very artistic, but I was able to sketch it with enough detail for an artist to draw it for me.

Since then, the image has taken on a life of its own. So what does this chain of rings represent? The Bible mentions chains more than thirty times. Sometimes they are used as a symbol of wealth and prosperity, as in the golden chains King Solomon made for God's temple (2 Chronicles 3:3–5). Other times, chains are part of imprisonment or captivity, like those that bound Peter in jail (Acts 12:6). Whenever verses about chains appear in the Bible, they are significant, and they always grab my attention.

When I first started thinking about the image, I was struck by the similarities and differences between my ring and God's. I realize that God's ring must be made of some divine material that is truly unbreakable. Mine is like one made of solid steel, a strong material that's very difficult to break with human hands. However, between those two rings—God's unbreakable ring and my smaller yet very strong one—are several smaller, thinner, weaker, and malleable rings linked together in the chain that connects God's ring to mine.

In my vision, God's mighty hand is stretching down from heaven, holding onto a massive, unbreakable ring formed by His love for us. His ring of love is connected to several smaller, weaker rings that ultimately connect to the ring I can hold onto. While I saw the last ring as my own, I interpret the vision to mean that each of us has our own ring forged by our love for God, our Creator.

My vision of the chain of rings linking us to God explains why it's so difficult to constantly and consistently live with faith, hope, love, conviction, purpose, intention, passion, meaning, peace, significance, satisfaction, and an attitude of gratitude that can lead to joy. It isn't any weakness on God's part. His love is unbreakable. But our own connection to His ring of love is fallible.

That is why we so often fall, sometimes even hitting rock bottom. The reason there is so much pain, suffering, and despair in the world is because of our weak connection to God. The weaker our chain links are between us and God, the less peace, joy, and satisfaction we will have in our lives. We are only as strong as our weakest link, our weakest connection to God.

Let's try to compare our chain that connects us to God to an individual athlete on a team. You can have the greatest quarterback in the world, but if the offensive center can't snap cleanly or protect the quarterback in the pocket, the entire play falls apart. Even the best quarterback needs receivers who can create space, separate from defenders, and make the catch. One weak link in the chain, and the whole team suffers.

It's no different in golf: you can crush a 300-yard drive, but if you can't sink the short putt when the pressure is on, the scorecard tells the truth. Strength in one area can't hide a breaking point in another. Once under pressure, your weakest link will break.

And that's the story of our spiritual lives, too. We can go to church, pray, and say all the right words—but if we lie at work, compromise at home, or deliberately walk outside God's design, then under stress, pressure, or temptation, that weak link snaps.

Our connection to God is like a chain: strong only when every link is aligned with Him. Broken links break people. Whole links strengthen families, restores marriages and brings lost children home.

We're All Sinners

For we must all appear before
the judgment seat of Christ.
(2 Corinthians 5:10 ESV)

As we explore the meaning of these rings, we will strive to understand the nature of this vision through God's words. Is this a divine image from God? At this point, I'm not entirely sure, but by the end of this book, I hope you'll see how it aligns with what the Bible teaches. My goal is to encourage you to put your trust in God and help you find answers to the question of what will happen when your body dies and what will then happen to your soul for all eternity.

Let's start by considering what the Bible says about sin and salvation. First, you have to acknowledge that you are a sinner—yes, you and I and every other person in this world. Whether you're two, fifty-two, or 102 years old, you are a sinner and have sinned because we've all sinned and fallen short of the glory of God (Romans 3:23).

Does that offend you? Maybe you're wondering who I am to judge others. In our society, *sin* is a loaded term, and judgment—calling someone a sinner—is definitely not appreciated. However, the key is recognizing that we're *all* sinners. It's not about judging others. It's just the truth and something we all know deep down.

If you've ever cared for a toddler, you've seen that from the moment even the sweetest baby begins to walk and talk, their selfish human nature manifests loudly and clearly. *Gimme,*

gimme, gimme . . . mine, mine, mine . . . watch me, watch me, watch me. From the beginning of our lives, we are innately self-centered people. We're born that way. Everything we do is about pleasing ourselves, and we believe the world revolves around us.

That's not all bad for babies and toddlers. They're vulnerable and need a lot of care and attention in order to thrive. Meeting their needs isn't wrong. It's necessary for their survival. But that is a stage of life we're meant to mature past and develop beyond—becoming less self-centered as we learn to care for others.

Unfortunately, some people never grow out of their childish ways and remain selfish throughout their lives. That leads to a tough life with significant ramifications for them and those around them.

God teaches us through the Bible that we are not the center of our universe. Instead, we learn that the entire universe revolves around God for all eternity. God created us to love Him and orient ourselves around Him, not our own selfish interests and desires.

Are lying and cheating falling short of God's plan for us? Yes. Is someone bigger and stronger beating up someone smaller and weaker also falling short? Yes. Are murder and rape falling short of God's plan? Yes.

Sometimes we try to make ourselves feel better by comparing our sins to those of others, calling them "bigger sinners." Some of us may sin less often or consider our own sins not as bad as the things others do. But take a look at the Ten Commandments. They aren't ranked from most important to least important; they are all equal.

People like to put us on the line and ask politically charged questions about what counts as sin. But as we saw in the examples above, we all know deep down inside what sin is. Is this what God intended for us? If not, it's most likely a sin—falling short or missing the mark of God's plan for us.

But make no mistake about it. As Jesus pointed out through the Gospels, no sin is greater than any other (John 8:7). Some sins may have greater consequences in our lives and the lives of others in this world, but no sinner is worse than or better than any other sinner.

For example, if you walked into a park and saw someone sitting on a bench pulling the legs off of insects for fun, you'd likely think it was strange, but you might just walk on by. However, if you saw someone hurting a puppy, you'd probably call the Humane Society or the police. What if someone was harming a child? You'd probably do everything you could to stop that person and rescue the child. You can see where perspective and judgment come into play in those situations. We care about who the victim is and how they are injured, and rightly so. Our actions have repercussions in our society.

But here's a question: How many rules does a child need to break in school to get in trouble? Only one, right?

How many laws does an adult have to break to be a lawbreaker? Just one.

How many crimes does a person need to commit to be a criminal? One.

So how many sins must a person commit to be a sinner? You know the answer. It's one.

The bottom line is that we're all sinners. We're all in the same boat. Each sin, from small to big, is enough to make us sinners. Very simply, sin is anything that falls short of God's intentions for us. The word for *sin* in Hebrew and Greek—the original languages of the Bible—means "missing the mark," like when an arrow falls short of the bull's-eye in archery.

We ultimately want to be the judge of our own lives and the jury of others around us. Once we start this comparison, it never stops. We often compare ourselves to others in various aspects of life, including status, job, house, car, finances, and relationships. God wants us to focus our lives on Him and stop judging each other from a worldly view.

When God searches our hearts, motives, and intentions, He focuses on our character and values. By His standard, we're all sinners. Any sin that God points out to us is for our own good. If we spend our lives falling short of His intentions for us, we'll never become truly satisfied, and we'll never have the relationship He planned for us while we're here on earth.

Every day—every minute—we have a choice to believe this simple truth or try to fight it. Fighting against the truth is a losing battle that causes immense frustration and pain in our lives. Our thoughts, choices, decisions, and behaviors either bring us closer to God or drive us farther away.

Salvation: The Already and the Not Yet

For it is by grace you have been saved,
through faith—and this is not from
yourselves, it is the gift of God—not
by works, so that no one can boast.
(Ephesians 2:8–9)

Since we are all sinners, how can we be saved? Some believe that their spouse, their children, their job, their money, a nice house, or a car will bring them satisfaction, peace, happiness, and joy. Others turn to outlets such as drugs, alcohol, and sex for satisfaction. But sadly, money and possessions do not bring lasting peace or joy. They can only offer momentary and fleeting superficial happiness. They will not save us or bring us peace.

The only peace, joy, and happiness that last are found in heaven. The Bible tells us that we can only enter heaven by having faith and trusting God, by accepting His salvation through His Son, Jesus Christ. We do not have to earn or work for God's love. We cannot work our way into heaven. As we see in Ephesians 2:8–9, salvation is a gift. We can't save ourselves.

We're all sinners, imperfect people in need of salvation. God is in heaven, perfect and holy. He wants us to be there with Him, but how can God let us into heaven with all our sin? If He just let us into heaven as we are with our sinful nature, we would bring gossip, envy, racism, jealousy, theft, pain, and other sinful parts of humanity with us into heaven.

Heaven is a perfect paradise. If God allowed us into heaven with all our character flaws, heaven wouldn't be perfect anymore.

It wouldn't be a paradise that you could remain in forever. It would actually become like hell, as on earth. So what does God have to do to allow us into heaven?

We must be made holy, suitable to live in heaven and in God's presence. This is all part of our salvation. It is helpful to view salvation as encompassing three aspects: past, present, and future. God's grace saves us through the life, death, and resurrection of Jesus Christ. Sin no longer has the same power over us (Romans 6:14). We are also in the process right now of being saved and sanctified, or made holy. God's Spirit is at work in our hearts, changing us and making us more like Christ (Galatians 2:20). One day when we die, our salvation will be complete. We will never sin—or want to—again (Philippians 1:6).

Part of that sanctifying process means we have to fix our weak, flimsy, broken links, by God's power and grace. It is not by works but through our mind, perspective, heart, feelings, emotions, and soul—our eternal selves—and the strength expressed in our actions and behavior that we develop a more godly character and can become more like Jesus. When Jesus's brother James talks about works (James 2:14–26), he's not saying that our works save us. He's telling us that we are called to actions that exemplify what Jesus did for our salvation. What actions are we responsible for? We're responsible for proactive thinking, perspective, worldview, and acceptance.

By acting and accepting, we will grow, and our spiritual maturity will blossom. Those actions will produce good fruits. We'll start to consistently think about Jesus and His supernatural helper—the Holy Spirit—and how he'll always be there to repair our broken connections and relationships, our direct fellowship and connection with God.

When there's sin in our lives, our relationship with God and most other aspects of our lives—especially the most important ones—fall apart under pressure. As tension is applied to a weak link, it will surely weaken more and most likely break.

Think about a marriage. When there is a conflict or deception, the harmony is strained, and stress rises. That causes tremendous pressure and tension in the connection between husband and wife. That leads to more stress, anger, anxiety, pain, and frustration with your other family members, your children, your coworkers, and countless others around you. How could other parts of your life work together in harmony when your relationship with your spouse is weakening or broken?

Now magnify that by infinity for all eternity. How can any part of your life be in harmony and fully satisfied when your relationship with your Creator—the Creator of the universe—is broken? God didn't create us to be in conflict with Him. God is holy, pure, and righteous. There's only one thing He can't do: He can't lie. His Word is always true because He *is* truth. He always does the right thing.

Heaven is perfect, a pure paradise. God wants us all to come into heaven with Him. That's the reason we were created. We have all sinned and broken our relationship with God. But He has made a way for us to be restored. If there were any other way for us to get into heaven, God would have made it available to us.

Jesus took on our sins to pay the price we could not pay. Jesus on the cross paid the highest penalty. He suffered torture, humiliation, rejection, and death. Jesus was rejected by God on the cross because Jesus took on all the sins of the world—every rape, every murder, every act of child abuse, every lie, every affair, and every broken heart—for us.

God is a righteous and just God. He's pure and holy, so He was unable to look upon Jesus on the cross. Jesus was separated from God on the cross and cried out, "My God, my God, why have you forsaken me?" (Matthew 27:46). If that doesn't break your heart, nothing will.

If we don't accept God's gift of mercy and forgiveness, Jesus will become our ultimate judge and not our advocate and Savior. If you're living a self-centered life, you're not in harmony with God. How could you not love and want to know more about the one who lived and died for you? How could we not live day by day in complete gratitude for our forgiveness? This is the good news: We can actually choose whether Jesus will be our ultimate judge at the end of our lives or our Savior. It's our choice.

The Coming Judgment

Everyone must die once, and
after that be judged by God.
(Hebrews 9:27 GNT)

When our bodies die, that's just the beginning of our eternal life. Death is only the beginning, not the end. Some people, if they are lucky, live more than ninety years, but what's that compared to all eternity? Is it worth continuing to live your life in the way of the world and gamble with all eternity?

You might find salvation at the very end of your life, as one of the criminals crucified next to Jesus did. When he turned to

Jesus in his final moments, he asked Him to remember him in heaven. Jesus replied to him, "I assure you: Today you will be with Me in paradise" (Luke 23:43 HCSB). This criminal had committed a crime that deserved judgment, which during those times meant execution. He lived the life of a criminal, but he was saved in his last minutes on earth. No one knows when their last day will come. I don't know if any of us will have the chance to receive salvation at our last breath. It's not worth the gamble.

I want to encourage you that you don't have to wait for your final moments on earth to keep from spending eternity in hell, separated from God our Creator. The moment you call out to God for help and admit that you've been living life for the wrong reasons, God will turn you to Jesus.

We must confess that we've been living by seeking help from all worldly sources and admit that Jesus is the answer to everything. The way He lived; the way He taught; the countless miracles that people witnessed Him do and then wrote down; the way He accepted being beaten, tortured, humiliated, and ultimately crucified—those things were all for those who would trust and accept Him as the Son of God.

Once you believe that fact, you are born again into God's family. That cannot be undone; we cannot be kicked out of God's family. That is wonderful news! But that's not all you receive from living as part of God's family. I also believe wholeheartedly that living a purpose-driven life with meaning, conviction, and passion for God and others will make your life on earth much more satisfying, joyful, and peaceful.

If we put God at the center of our lives, everything else will find its rightful place. However, we need to examine ourselves first and make sure we're not thinking we're better than our neighbors. We should only compare ourselves to Jesus who lived a perfect, sinless life. If we follow His lead inch by inch, step by step, and day by day, we may have some chance of living at peace, being satisfied, and feeling a very real, close, personal connection to God.

The Bible doesn't tell us exactly how to humble ourselves, but it does often encourage us to be humble and live our lives with humility. The message boils down to this: Humility is not about thinking less of yourself. It's simply thinking *about* yourself less and more about God and those around you, putting their needs first.

The sooner we realize that we're all in the same boat, the easier it will be for us to live more with compassion and mercy. We must recognize that some individuals face extremely challenging lives. They've suffered greatly, and some of those people unfortunately live very bitter and resentful lives. We need to be compassionate toward them because people who are hurting tend to hurt others around them without even realizing it. As the saying goes, "Hurt people hurt people."

People who are hurting are almost hoping and wishing for death. They think that once they die, that's it; it's the end of them, and their pain and misery will stop. But that isn't true. As Hebrews 9:27 tells us, each of us will stand before God's judgment seat. Heaven is real. Hell is real. We will spend eternity in one or the other. So choose now who you are going to serve (Joshua 24:15) before it's too late.

Strengthening Weakened Links

No matter how deep the stain of your
sins, I can take it out and make you
as clean as freshly fallen snow.
(Isaiah 1:18 TLB)

In the book of Romans, Paul tells us that nothing can separate us from God's love through Jesus (Romans 8:38–39)—not what others do to us, not our own sins, not our weak and broken links that connect us to God. However, the next chapters will explore how our fellowship and connection with God can be damaged by sin, even for believers who are eternal members of God's chosen family.

At times, our family connection may seem strained or fragile, but our relationship remains strong through Jesus. We're merely one small damaged link away from returning to God's perfect connection and fellowship.

The secret to maintaining a supernaturally strong connection with the Creator of the universe lies in His divine Word. The more we study, ingest, meditate, and feel God's Word with our heart and soul, the stronger our connection with God becomes.

If we want to be spiritually healthy, we must feed on God's divine Word and His will. Our eyes are the lens to our souls. If we watch trashy content, our minds, our thinking, and our perspective will start to look trashy and get influenced in a negative, ungodly way. The content we consume through media or the Internet has a tremendous influence on our perception of reality and our worldview. Always ask yourself, *What is my perspective on a particular situation?* Is the world, media outlets, and news shaping my view, or is it God's Word? Garbage in, garbage out. If we keep filling our minds and bodies with things that hurt us physically, emotionally, and spiritually, it's nearly impossible to live a God-centered life.

Just as children want everything they want, when and how they want it, so do adults. God as a loving parent isn't going to give us things that He knows will hurt us. Would you? Would you give your child everything they asked for? Of course not. No loving parent would ever let their child do everything they wanted[3] (except maybe Veruca's dad in *Charlie and the Chocolate Factory*).

Think about it. Children want to run into the street, climb things too high, try to touch hot things, play with sharp objects, and eat only junk food. Why? Because they don't know what's best for them. The same is true for us in our relationship with God, our Father.

Jesus explained to His disciples:

> Which of you, if your son asks for bread, will give him a stone? Or if he asks for a fish, will give him a snake? If you, then, though you are evil, know how to give good gifts to your children, how much more will your Father in heaven give good gifts to those who ask him! (Matthew 7:9–11)

God can see everything, every detail. He's not constrained by space and time. If you ask for something from God, He'll either say yes, no, or not yet. But He will only give His children good gifts. He wants the best for us.

Over time, loving parents gradually let their children take on more responsibility as they mature. As parents, we want to give our children good gifts, especially when they listen to us.

The more we study God's Word, the stronger our grip on our connection with Him will become. If we only read God's Word once in a while, that's like holding onto one of our chain links with our little pinky. If we study it twice a month, that's like holding onto our connection with two fingers. But if we study God's Word daily, that's like holding onto our connection with God with the strongest grip we have, using all five fingers, our palm, and our muscles.

Unfortunately, even with our greatest strength, there will be times when our grip loosens, our palms start to sweat, or our muscles just get fatigued. When that happens, it's usually during some of life's most trying times relationally, financially, physically, or emotionally. During those times, you may feel like your connection to God is broken and you're just free-falling through the sky, hopeless.

When you're flat on your back and the only thing to do is look up, you see God. Even during your darkest hour, all you need to do is look up to God for help and ask for a Savior. That's when Jesus is there again and again to catch us out of thin air. He'll continue to rescue us for the rest of our lives if we let him. He'll always be there for us, holding us, comforting us, and spending time with us as we repair broken and weak chain links together.

The purpose of this book is to give you hope, encouragement, and insight into some complex topics in the Bible. As you will see, I've benefited from an array of different pastors and theologians from many different schools of thought. Some are old-school conservatives, some are progressives, and others are middle-of-the-road.

It is not my intention to battle over Scripture interpretation or necessarily insist on one view or another. Many theologians will tell you there is really only one proper interpretation of the Bible. Still, there can be several different methods of delivering the message to people, especially when it comes to practical application. It's amazing to read Scripture from thousands of years ago that seems more relevant today than ever before.[4]

My goal by the end of this book is for every reader to walk away with a deeper understanding of the vision I had and how it makes sense of some of life's most difficult challenges. Hopefully, my vision will help explain why it's so difficult to feel good about ourselves, even when we're trying to do what's best, what's right, and what's just.

This book is written explicitly for individuals seeking more out of life. It's for those who constantly feel like they fail too often despite their best efforts and intentions. These true seekers are simply trying to live faithfully and honestly. I will do my absolute best to fill each chapter with God's love, grace, and mercy. In the next chapter, we will explore what the Bible teaches us about love—God's love for us and our love for Him.

God's Love

See what great love the Father has lavished on
us, that we should be called children of God!
(1 John 3:1)

What is the most important commandment in the Bible?

The religious leaders in Jerusalem asked Jesus that question. Do you know what His answer was?

Jesus replied: "Love the Lord your God with all your heart and with all your soul and with all your mind. This is the first and greatest commandment. And the second is like it: Love your neighbor as yourself." (Matthew 22:37–39)

Love. Love is the most important thing we're told to do in the Bible. Love God and love others. The entire Bible comes down to that.

Love is central to the Bible. It's the heart of the gospel, the good news of salvation. It's the cornerstone of creation and the foundation of our relationship with God. As the Bible says, "God *is* love" (emphasis added) (1 John 4:8). Everything revolves around this truth.

That's why the chain in my vision begins and ends with love. God's love forms the strongest ring that links the others to us. Our love for God connects us to the chain. The rest of the rings are forged and maintained by Jesus's self-sacrificial love and the work of the Spirit.

It may seem odd to talk about love as a commandment. After all, we're more used to love as an emotion or a feeling. But love is more than how we feel about others. It's conveyed through actions.

Consider a man who tells his wife he loves her every day. Sounds nice, right? But what if he never spends any time with her, never does anything thoughtful for her, and only occasionally kisses her? His wife would have good reason to doubt that he means it when he says he loves her.

No one wants to be in a relationship with someone who only *says* but never *does*. The same is true with our relationship with God. He wants us to have the deepest, most intimate relationship with us. God isn't interested in an emotionally fleeting relationship like a grade-school crush. He wants us to choose to love, honor, and respect Him with every thought, action, and consideration.

God doesn't want an experiential relationship that is based on how we feel that day. Any mature married couple will tell you that a strong, loving, caring, and honoring marriage takes work, dedication, and a willingness to prioritize each other, to put your spouse's needs before your own.

God demonstrates His love for us in all He has done and continues to do for us, and He wants us to demonstrate our love for Him and for others.

God's Love for Us

Give thanks to the LORD, for he is good!
His faithful love endures forever.
(Psalm 136:1 NLT)

God's love for us is so grand and expansive that it's difficult for us to comprehend it. The Bible is full of real-life accounts and events that express God's love, grace, and mercy. The Psalms describe God's unfailing love and compassion (Psalm 51:1). The Hebrew word often used in these verses is *hesed*, which means "lovingkindness, mercy, steadfast love, loyalty, faithfulness."[5] Psalm 136 repeats over and over that God's love endures forever.

Eternal, unending love is a hard concept for our human minds to understand. I believe that one day when we're standing in front of the Almighty God, the Creator of heaven and earth, we will develop a better understanding of God's love for us. I believe our minds will be transformed and not constrained by space and time. For now, we get glimpses of God's power and His supernatural abilities throughout the Bible.

Praise be to the God and Father of our Lord Jesus Christ, who has blessed us in the heavenly realms with every spiritual blessing in Christ. For He chose us in Him before the creation of the world to be holy and blameless in His sight. In love, He predestined us for adoption to sonship through Jesus Christ, in accordance with His pleasure and will—to the praise of His glorious grace, which He has freely given us in the One He loves. In him, we have redemption through his blood, the forgiveness of sins, in accordance with the riches of God's grace that He lavished on us. (emphasis added) (Ephesians 1:3–8)

These verses describe how much God loves us. He planned for us even before He laid down the world's foundation. God made earth for us to live on. God wanted more people in His family and chose us to be His sons and daughters. God's entire focus is on us. Each moment, God knows every thought, feeling, emotion, pain, tear, and hair on our head.

In the Psalms, King David writes about God's love: "You keep track of all my sorrows. You have collected all my tears in your bottle. You have recorded each one in your book" (Psalm 56:8 NLT). The prophet Isaiah records God's promises: "I'd never forget you—never. Look, I've written your names on the backs of my hands" (Isaiah 49:15–16 MSG). Jesus told His disciples not to worry because God would care for even the smallest details in their lives: "Indeed, the very hairs of your head are all numbered" (Luke 12:7 NASB1995).

How amazing is it to know that the Creator of the universe knows how many hairs are on each of our heads, or how many tears we have cried in our lifetime? Again, these are things that our human brains cannot fully comprehend. God's love is so far-reaching and supernatural that we can only get veiled reflections of it in God's words that were given to us so we can know Him. God shows us what true love is. His very nature is love.

God promises that He will never stop loving us and that nothing in this world or the next can separate us from Him. The apostle Paul explained:

> For I am convinced that neither death nor life, neither angels nor demons, neither the present nor the future, nor any powers, neither height nor depth, nor anything else in all creation, will be able to separate us from the love of God that is in Christ Jesus our Lord. (Romans 8:38–39)

God's love is unconditionally eternal. God's love doesn't come with limitations like *if*, *but*, or *when*. God doesn't just love you *if* or *when* you do *this* or *that*. God's love is based solely on who He is—His nature—not on what we've done. There is nothing you can do to make God love you less, and there's nothing you can do to make God love you more.

In the Bible, God calls us His masterpieces (Ephesians 2:10). Your parents might not have planned you, but God did. There are no accidental children (although there are plenty of accidental parents). God created everything with a purpose. His purpose is that we love and serve Him and those around us.

Whether we realize it or not, we each have a ministry (think of it as a calling or mission), our contribution to the world. Everyone has their own unique qualities that add value to others and the world. One day we'll give an account to God about how we fulfilled our ministry—our purpose for being who He created us to be—and the times when we acted and behaved how He made us to be.

Every one of us is unique, but we are all loved by God.

Jesus's Love for Us

For God so loved the world that
he gave his one and only Son, that
whoever believes in him shall not
perish but have eternal life.
(John 3:16)

The greatest demonstration of God's love for us is found in Jesus. God loves us enough to want to be with us forever, despite our sins against Him and others. He loves us enough to send His only Son to live a human life; to suffer; to feel pain, torment, and torture; to teach us how to live; and to save us from our sins. Jesus lived the perfect life. He lived the life we should be living. He died the death we earned. Jesus rose from the dead, ascended into heaven, and sent back the all-powerful Holy Spirit to be with us always and forever. We'll never find a greater love.

The Bible is all about Jesus. He is the beginning and the end— the Alpha and the Omega (Revelation 22:13). In Colossians, Paul wrote about Jesus's centrality as the Son of God:

> The Son is the image of the invisible God, the firstborn over all creation. For in him all things were created: things in heaven and on earth, visible and invisible, whether thrones or powers or rulers or authorities; all things have been created through him and for him. He is before all things, and in him all things hold together. (Colossians 1:15–17)

Everything was created by Him, through Him, and for Him. But His divinity, majesty, and glory did not stop Him from becoming just like us, except without sin (Hebrews 4:15). Jesus is Immanuel—God with us (Matthew 1:23).

We are told in Philippians that Jesus willingly gave up all His privileges to be born, live, suffer, and die for us.

> Though he was God, he did not think of equality with God as something to cling to. Instead, he gave up his divine privileges; he took the humble position of a slave and was born as a human being. When he appeared in human form, he humbled himself in obedience to God and died a criminal's death on a cross. Therefore, God elevated him to the place of highest honor and gave him the name above all other names, that at the name of Jesus every knee should bow, in heaven and on earth and under the earth, and every tongue declare that Jesus Christ is Lord, to the glory of God the Father. (Philippians 2:6–11 NLT)

Many people will, unfortunately, miss heaven by about eighteen inches—the distance from their head to their heart. What I mean is that most people in the world believe there's a God. For this book, I'm going to assume that you believe in God and that you've likely read and heard about all the miracles Jesus did while He was on earth. If not, I recommend one of my favorite books that verifies Jesus's teachings, miracles, and especially His resurrection, *A Case for Christ* by Lee Strobel.[6]

As a well-known journalist, Strobel made his name uncovering myths, frauds, and deceptions. He went on a mission to uncover and disprove Christianity, or at least raise some doubts about the facts. He researched the resurrection story, using his vast resources and connections to poke some holes in the account.

Strobel knew that if the resurrection never really happened, he could reduce Jesus to a martyr or just another prophet. To Strobel's amazement, he found overwhelming evidence of Jesus's death, crucifixion, and resurrection. Reading his book should remove any doubt you have about Jesus's resurrection. The historical facts are solid.

Many people also believe that a man named Jesus really lived and died about 2,000 years ago. But they believe these are just facts that remain in their heads, not in their hearts.

We all need to remember what the Bible says about this kind of head knowledge: "You say you have faith, for you believe that there is one God. Good for you! Even the demons believe this, and they tremble in terror" (James 2:19 NLT). This verse tells us that even the devil, demons, and evil creatures believe in God and know Jesus is the Son of God and what his goals are. *But you will not find any of these creatures in heaven.*

Just because we know about God and Jesus (as the demons do) doesn't mean we will go to heaven. We need to love, trust, and commit our lives to Jesus with our hearts. The Bible tells us, "If you declare with your mouth, 'Jesus is Lord,' and believe in your heart that God raised him from the dead, you will be saved" (Romans 10:9).

What does it mean to confess that Jesus is Lord? In biblical and ancient times, a lord was a master or boss. To confess that Jesus is Lord and master of your life, you first have to repent of your sins and humble yourself before Him. Admit the things you've done wrong, submit and surrender your old ways to Him, and then make a commitment to follow His ways, not your ways.

God promises in the Bible to forgive us when we repent and confess our sins. "If we confess our sins, he is faithful and just and will forgive us our sins and purify us from all unrighteousness" (1 John 1:9). In Romans, we learn that "God says he will accept and acquit us—declare us 'not guilty'—if we trust Jesus Christ to take away our sins. And we all can be saved in this same way, by coming to Christ, no matter who we are or what we have been like" (Romans 3:22 TLB). Jesus will never turn a repentant sinner away.

Jesus *accepts* us as we are but loves us too much to *leave* us in our sinful ways. If we went to Jesus with our temptations more often, we'd have fewer sins to confess. Think about it. If we turned to Jesus every time we were tempted with lust, greed, envy, or many other sins, we'd sin much less often.

Being tempted isn't a sin, but it is a reminder that we need God's help to live our lives like Jesus. Remember, Jesus was tempted during His time on earth. But he always prayed and used God's Word to ward off temptations. For every sin, there's a scripture. For every temptation, there's a verse.

If you accepted Jesus as your eternal Savior, you can never be separated from God's love. If you want to live a better life while on earth, it's best to surrender your selfish desires and follow Jesus's teachings and views on everything.

The more we study Jesus, the more we will look and act like him. When you know and love someone really well, you start to speak, act, behave, and even look like them. As we start acting like Jesus at home, at work, and in our communities, people will start to notice. We will stand out because if we follow Jesus, we won't want to go to certain places, do certain things, or say hurtful things. Following Jesus is key to keeping the strongest connection to our heavenly Father.

Our Love for God

I have loved you even as the Father
has loved me. Remain in my love.
(John 15:9 NLT)

For most believers, their love ring for God the Father is strong. Depending on where they are on their journey, some may have a nearly unbreakable connection to God, while others have a smaller, more fragile ring that represents their love for God. Many newer believers have an easier time focusing on Jesus, the Son of God, than on God the Father and the Holy Spirit, the great Counselor.

I believe God sent Jesus to us, to live among us, eat with us, struggle with us, feel pain like us, and teach us how to live. Jesus ultimately lived the perfect sinless life—the life we should live—dying the death we should have died, and being raised from the grave. God the Father sent Jesus to us to make Himself more understandable and relatable to all of us. We should be grateful that God sent Jesus at a time when people were recording documents, when scribes were active, and when ingenuity, innovation, and the building blocks of today's technology were beginning to form.

What I've just recently started to realize is that the closer I move to Jesus, the stronger my relationship is with Him and the more I start to understand God the Father and the all-powerful

Holy Spirit. Truth be told, I still have a long way to go before I will be confident telling people that I have a mature and solid understanding of God the Father and the Holy Spirit. To be honest, I still feel at times that I'm only beginning my life journey of understanding.

For those who want to go to heaven, who love, honor, respect, and fear God, our best chance is to put all our hope, trust, and faith in Jesus and try to mirror the way He thought, worked, lived, and loved. Many Christians say and wear bracelets that say WWJD (What Would Jesus Do). When we mess up, Jesus will be right there holding us, comforting us, and protecting us from falling too far. I picture Him holding me up in His arms, guiding me, and showing me how to fix and repair damaged, weak, or broken links that connect me to God's love. Jesus gives us the tools, the manual, the GPS, and the road map to fix our connection to God.

The very first thing every one of us must do is confess to Jesus that we're broken, confused, and unsatisfied. Tell Jesus that you know He knows all the sins you've ever committed and will commit in the future, and that you want to live a better life. You want to live a life that attempts to please Jesus. Then you need to invite Him into your heart and ask Him to take over every area of your life, not just all the parts that you think need fixing but everything—a complete surrender.

Once you submit and surrender to Jesus and truly have a change of heart, you're saved just like that—in that instant.

Jesus will never leave us or abandon us. It's during the most challenging periods in our lives that Jesus is knocking at our door. He wants us to let Him in so He can comfort us, protect us, and teach us how to truly live with peace, grace, mercy, compassion, and love in every situation.

Unfortunately, many Christians feel like God is distant or is allowing them to go through the furnace all alone. Again, this is because many have an emotional relationship with God. They are basing their relationship with God on how they're feeling at the moment, like a middle-school crush. When we build our lives with Jesus as the foundation, none of life's trials or storms can wash us or our relationship with God away.

Sometimes God needs to put us through difficulties so we grow, develop, and learn to lean on Him. The book of Job in the Old Testament tells the story of a believer whom God allowed Satan to test. Job uses the imagery of gold being purified by fire, saying that "when he tests me, I will come out as pure as gold" (Job 23:10 NLT).

When God allows us to walk through the fiery furnace, He's refining us to make us as pure as gold. Before jewelry makers work with gold, they have to remove any non-pure metals. They need to burn off any impurities. Once the gold is purified, it can be poured into the mold to form a masterpiece.

How does a jeweler know when the gold is pure? He knows it is pure when he can see his own reflection in the gold. That's what God wants for us. He wants to burn off all our impurities (sin) and make us pure so He can see His image in us. After all, we're made in God's image, created to love God and serve Him.

Even though sin has blurred God's image in us, Jesus heals everything. We don't know that God is all we need until God is all we have. Most people feel closest to God when they are most desperate and don't know where else to turn or who else to reach out to. Sometimes it's not until we're flat on our backs and there's nowhere else to look that we finally look up toward heaven. Thankfully, God specializes in heart transplants, changing us to be holy and righteous like Him.

How Should We Live Then?

Since you have been raised to new
life with Christ, set your sights on the
realities of heaven, where Christ sits in
the place of honor at God's right hand.
(Colossians 3:1 NLT)

God is always in control. He's the initiator and maintainer of our relationship. The reason for everything we do comes from God. It started at birth with our first breath, our food, clothing, warmth, nourishment, safety, protection, resources, health, jobs, and more. He gave us all those things. In response, we seek to give back to Him. We try to give back our time, talents, and treasures.

The very reason we pray and seek God is because He spoke to us first through communication with our forefathers in the faith and through His Word—the Bible. Prayer should start with listening to God. We first read His Word, study it, digest it, and meditate on it. By doing so, God will always speak to you first, and you will be able to listen. Just like any good communicator or relationship, the more you listen and pay attention to the one speaking, the more you grow toward and with that person.

The prophet Daniel wrote, "Then I turned my face to the Lord God, seeking him" (Daniel 9:3 ESV). By turning our faces toward God, we'll hear Him, and we'll understand His plan and purpose for us. We'll realize that He's a good God who loves and helps us. He knows what's best for us.

God is always in control, but there is some action required on our part. That is where the chain link connection comes into play. We have the responsibility to pray, seek, and ask God for our hearts' desires and ultimately receive God's grace, mercy, love, and forgiveness. That strengthens our connection to Him.

The Bible uses a building metaphor to describe our spiritual connection to God through Jesus. A brick or stone by itself can't do anything to hold up a building. But stones placed on top of each other can make a solid foundation, with Jesus as the cornerstone.

> …built on the foundation of the apostles and prophets, with Christ Jesus himself as the chief cornerstone. In him the whole building is joined together and rises to become a holy temple in the Lord. And in him you too are being built together to become a dwelling in which God lives by his Spirit.. (Ephesians 2:20–22)

We're like the stones and bricks that must lean on Jesus. Together with other believers, we help and support each other in our spiritual growth and connection to God. God loves variety. Look at how He made us all. Each and every one of us is important, significant, and necessary to God's plan.

If the building's walls, ceiling joists, and beams are disconnected from the frame and foundation, the entire building will collapse or implode when a storm comes. It's the same for us. If we're not relying on Jesus and are disconnected from God, we won't be able to stand firm when a bad situation or circumstance arises.

Another metaphor the Bible uses to describe our relationship with Jesus and other believers is a body (1 Corinthians 12). We are all different parts that make up a strong spiritual body, with Jesus as our head. We're all unique. Some of us are more prominent or influential in the world than others, but we're all significant body parts that make up God's Kingdom here on earth.

We're all part of one body. If one body part is disconnected, it could die and endanger the rest of the body. If your ear, nose, finger, or toe is cut off from your body, you probably won't die, but that body part sure will. If you lose a leg, arm, or vital organ, not only does that part of the body die, but you're at serious risk of killing the rest of the body as well.

When you're not spiritually connected to God, everything will eventually fall apart: marriage, children, finances, work, career, and meaningful relationships. You ultimately will start to wither and die because you're not connected to Jesus.

Our connection to Jesus is also described as a vine with many branches. Jesus told His disciples, "Live in me, and I will live in you. A branch cannot produce any fruit by itself. It has to stay attached to the vine. In the same way, you cannot produce fruit unless you live in me" (John 15:4 GW).

What kind of fruit does Jesus want us to produce when we're connected to His vine and part of His body? As we saw in Galatians, "The fruit of the Spirit is love, joy, peace, forbearance, kindness, goodness, faithfulness, gentleness and self-control" (Galatians 5:22–23). It's impossible to bear this fruit consistently and live with purpose and passion if you're not connected to the vine—Jesus.

If you're bearing the fruit of the Holy Spirit, that means you have a strong relationship with Jesus and a strong connection with God. It doesn't mean you won't still struggle with sin and temptation.

We can't always control our feelings. We can't always control temptations or emotions, but we can control our perspective and how it influences our response. Like I heard a pastor once say, "I can't keep the birds from flying over my head, but I can stop them from making a nest in my hair." If we're able to control our thinking and have a better, more Christ-like perspective on situations and circumstances, we should be in a better position to influence our actions and behavior, which will lead to better character.

Maybe you wonder, like I do, what happens to the folks who "tried" to live the life Jesus wants them to live but ended up going right back to living sinful lives. The answer is I'm not sure, and I don't want to find out the hard way. I pray that some of the things in this book will help you think a little more deeply about your character, integrity, perspective, behavior, and relationship with Jesus.

There's a story that when Charlemagne's soldiers were baptized, they wouldn't allow their swords to go underneath the water. They would stretch out their arms and hold their swords extended above the water while every other body part was submerged and baptized. What they were saying was, in effect, that God could have every part of them except their swords, knowing they would do things with their swords that wouldn't please God.

I wonder how many people still do that today. Do we act like Jesus at church but not at work? Do we act like Jesus during Bible study but not at home? Do we act like Jesus in small groups but not out with our old college friends?

What about the less obvious parts of our lives? What else are we trying to hold back from God (like the soldiers' swords)? Do we hold back our marriages, families, in-laws, jobs, or finances? Why would we trust God with our souls and all of eternity but not trust Him with our money and relationships?

What are we keeping above the water and not trusting to God?

God won't bless all our lives if we hold things back from Him. We can't ask God to bless our careers and our finances if we're holding them back from Him. Many Christians are quick to confess to God that their children are lost or out of control and offer them up to God. "Here, God, please help my children. If they are lost, please bring them back." But we're often slow or distant with the things in our lives that we think we don't need help with.

We have to remember that God doesn't just want a religion with you. He wants a relationship with you through Jesus. As the Bible tells us, God sent His Son to redeem us. We have been adopted as children of God (Galatians 4:5–7).

That brings us full circle. As the Bible says, "We love, because He first loved us" (1 John 4:19 NASB1995). We're created to be branches, always connected to God through Jesus as the living vine. Whenever we break away or become disconnected from our vine, we not only won't bear the fruit of the Holy Spirit but will wither and die.

In the next chapters, we will look at how sin weakens the links connecting us to God and what we can do to strengthen our relationship with God.

Sin, Guilt, and Forgiveness

For everyone has sinned; we all fall short of God's

glorious standard.

(Romans 3:23 NLT)

S in is not a popular topic in our society, at least not in the sense we're talking about in this chapter. When most people hear the word *sin*, their eyes glaze over and they lose interest in the conversation. Or they get uncomfortable and look for the quickest exit. Unless you're in church or Sunday school, few people expect a discussion about sin. But sin is everywhere around us.

It's not often called sin, but it's all over the news. It's in movies and television shows. We see it on social media and in magazines, books, and newspapers. We talk about it all the time.

We're confronted with it and its consequences every day. But we don't often take it seriously.

Sin is a punchline. We treat it like a joke, something to laugh at. We use it to describe good food or luxurious items. Have you ever said something was "sinfully delicious" or "sinfully soft"? The media we consume encourages us to trivialize, minimize, and mock the very idea of sin.

Said another way, we're taught to laugh at or scoff at the same things Jesus willingly died on the cross for. That is exactly what Satan's goal is: to numb us to the actions and behaviors that put Jesus on the cross. Rarely does our culture highlight how destructive sinful actions are or the awful consequences they have on families and others around us. Sin has many life-changing consequences.

Sin separates us from God our Creator: "It is your evil that has separated you from your God. Your sins cause him to turn away from you, so he does not hear you" (Isaiah 59:2 NCV). Sin creates estrangement between you, God, and others around you—but especially God. God is holy, pure, and true, and we're not.

Sin also causes enormous amounts of pressure, stress, and anxiety in our lives. Sin creates guilt, whether you recognize it or not. In the Psalms, King David wrote, "My guilt has overwhelmed me like a burden too heavy to bear" (Psalm 38:4). Because we're created to follow God's commands, whenever we're doing the opposite, we're out of harmony with God, ourselves, and others.

Sin condemns us. When we're at odds and constantly fighting what God planned for us, we'll lose sleep, we'll be a ball of stress, and we won't be able to think straight or make wise choices. We'll be snappy, short-tempered, and unpleasant to be around. Our own sinful thoughts, actions, and behavior condemn us and keep us estranged from God. King David tells us, "God is a righteous judge and always condemns the wicked" (Psalm 7:11 GNT).

Sin weakens the links that connect us to God. Each link symbolizes our connection to God. As sin takes root in our lives, our connection with God is strained. Individual sins on their own will not make us fall very far from God. If one of our links is bending under pressure, we may be able to recognize the need to repair it or replace it with a stronger link.

We are all sinners who have sinned and will sin again, even with our best intentions. Because of the very nature of humans, this is unavoidable. However, the good news is that once we identify those sins early on, we can isolate them like a toxic cancer, address the sinful actions, or cut them out of our lives completely.

Knowing that we all sin, our main goal is to work hard on strengthening our connection to God so we never have to fall too far from Him. In this chapter, we will explore how to recognize the weakening of one of our connections to God, what to do about it, and how to repair it right away.

What Is Sin?

Everyone who sins breaks God's
law, because sin is the same
as breaking God's law.
(1 John 3:4 CEV)

What is sin? How does the Bible define it? As we mentioned earlier, sin means "to miss the mark." Like in archery, when an arrow falls short of the target, it misses the mark. Sin is anything we do that fails to hit the target of God's commandments.

As the saying goes, there's an "i" in the middle of sin. At the root of sin is our self-centered pride, which encourages sinful thoughts and desires. And those sinful thoughts and desires lead to sinful actions and behaviors.

It's important to remember what the Apostle Paul explained about sin: We *all* sin because we *all* have fallen short and have missed the mark (Romans 3:23). This discussion about sin is not about pointing fingers. We're all in the same boat. Only Jesus lived a life without sinning.

Many sins are hard to avoid, but with proper recognition and detection, we can arm ourselves and do our best to prevent our sinful tendencies from leading to sinful actions. Let's look at some ways the Bible describes sin.

In the Old Testament book of Exodus, we have the account of God giving the Ten Commandments to Moses (Exodus 20, 34). When Moses met with God on Mount Sinai, God spoke to him saying, "The LORD, the LORD God, merciful and gracious, longsuffering, and abounding in goodness and truth, keeping mercy for thousands, forgiving iniquity and transgression and sin" (Exodus 34:6–7 NKJV). Some commentators point out the three words used to describe what God forgives: iniquity, transgression, and sin.[7]

Starting with sin, we see in the Bible two types of sins. First, we have sins of commission. Those are sins we commit by doing something that God's law forbids. Consider the Ten

Commandments: "You must not murder. You must not commit adultery. You must not steal. You must not testify falsely against your neighbor. You must not covet your neighbor's house" (Exodus 20:13–17 NLT). Those commands give us specific instructions not to lie, steal, kill, cheat on our spouses, or sinfully want what is not ours.

Next are sins of omission. We commit those sins by *not* doing something that God's law commands us to do. We can also find examples of them in the Ten Commandments. "Remember to observe the Sabbath day by keeping it holy. Honor your father and mother" (Exodus 20:8, 12 NLT). In the New Testament, James tells us, "Remember, it is sin to know what you ought to do and then not do it" (James 4:17 NLT).

Another word the Bible uses to describe sin is *transgression*. In the Psalms, King David tells us, "Blessed is the one whose transgression is forgiven, whose sin is covered" (Psalm 32:1 ESV). The word *transgression* means "rebellion or revolt."[8]

Transgressions are actions that are rebellions against God. They are boundaries that are broken. Using a sports metaphor, think of choosing to go out of bounds on purpose versus staying within the playing field lines.

Finally, we see that God forgives iniquity. The word *iniquity* can also be translated as "guilt, fault, or perversity."[9] Iniquity is premeditated, continuing sinful action and can escalate. Iniquity is sin at its worst.

This type of sin may start small with lust or desire, which may seem unavoidable. Allowed to continue, lust can turn into a transgression when we begin to act on the desire. Eventually, the sinful actions become a pattern of iniquity, allowing sin to take shape in our hearts, minds, actions, and behavior. That can lead to adultery, rape, incest, murder, and many other horrific actions that occur daily throughout the world.

As we can see, sin is no laughing matter. It's deadly serious. When you find yourself laughing at sinful behavior, examine what lies you're being told about sin.

Hypocrisy, Shame, and Guilt

Such people claim they know God, but
they deny him by the way they live.
(Titus 1:16 NLT)

Sin is at the center of each one of our broken links. What does that look like in our lives? The Bible gives us a picture of a sinful life.

When you follow your own wrong inclinations, your lives will produce these evil results: impure thoughts, eagerness for lustful pleasure, idolatry, spiritism (that is, encouraging the activity of demons), hatred and fighting, jealousy and anger, constant effort to get the best for yourself, complaints and criticisms, the feeling that everyone else is wrong except those in your own little group—and there will be wrong doctrine, envy, murder, drunkenness, wild parties, and all that sort of thing. (Galatians 5:19–21 TLB)

In the Apostle Paul's letter to Timothy, he describes what living in a sinful culture is like.

For people will love only themselves and their money. They will be boastful and proud, scoffing at God, disobedient to their parents, and ungrateful. They will consider nothing sacred. They will be unloving and unforgiving; they will slander others and have no self-control. They will be cruel and hate what is good. They will betray their friends, be reckless, be puffed up with pride, and love pleasure rather than God. They will act religious, but they will reject the power that could make them godly. (2 Timothy 3:2–5 NLT)

Those descriptions sound pretty familiar, don't they? They could be reporting on life in twenty-first century America. Living sinful lives brings pain, sadness, and destruction to our existence, our relationships with others, and our connection with God.

Notice that sinful actions include acting or pretending to be religious while rejecting God and His power to make real change in our lives. It's a kind of hypocrisy, similar to when we claim to be Christians but don't act like it all the time.

Do you act differently around different people? Are you one person around your family and another person around your old school friends? Do you behave differently when you're in church than when you're at work? That's hypocrisy.

The Greek word *hupokrités* refers to an actor on stage wearing a mask, playing different characters and acting out.[10] That is where we get our word *hypocrite*. So when we "play" different people in different settings, wearing masks that hide who we really are, we're being hypocritical.

We don't like being called hypocrites. Many people try to excuse their behavior by claiming, "This is just how I am." Others take it a step further and say, "This is how God made me."

The truth is that God did not create us to be two-faced, double-minded, or hypocritical. We often behave that way for many reasons stemming from worldly influences and prior experiences. We have a strong desire to be accepted and approved by others. That spurs us to be hypocrites because we're convinced that we need to act a certain way to impress others around us.

The problem is that living multiple lives leads to having a split soul. We end up so divided against ourselves that we never have peace. We can never be truly satisfied living that way. Division brings lies, compromise, destruction, and death. Those lead to shame or guilt.

Have you ever considered that feeling guilty could actually be good for us? Shame makes us turn inward. It leads to resentment, poor self-worth, and low self-esteem. Feeling shameful tells us, "I'm a bad person." Shame does not lead us to repentance and faith in Jesus.

Guilt, on the other hand, is God-given. Guilt tells us, "I *did* a bad thing." God wired us to have those emotions and feelings to let us know we've messed up. The feeling of guilt is what naturally draws us to our Savior, Jesus. When we focus on our shame, we minimize what Jesus did for us. He died for our sins *and* shame.

A feeling of guilt is true because we are all guilty. We can live a courageous and honest life when we recognize our guilt and repent of our sins. Because we are all sinners living in a fallen world with other sinners, we're constantly bombarded by sin and its consequences.

On our own, the situation would be hopeless. We would be permanently separated from God, our connection irreparably broken. That's why we need a Savior—Jesus.

Jesus lived a perfect life, without sin. He died for our sins and took our punishment. In return, Jesus gives us all His sinless righteousness. The Apostle Paul explains, "God made him who had no sin to be sin for us, so that in him we might become the righteousness of God" (2 Corinthians 5:21 NIV). Jesus is the only one who can help us reconnect with God, our Father.

Having these feelings is the first step toward repentance, turning away from our sinful ways. A change of heart will ultimately lead to restoration, peace, and satisfaction. That is what broken links are all about.

We must do something. Accepting Jesus, accepting His forgiveness and grace, takes action on our part. When someone gives you a present, you must act. You can either accept it or reject it. When someone gives you a gift, you need to take the time to unwrap the gift. It's a physical, mental, and emotional exercise just to receive and accept a gift from a family member or friend.

Accepting the gift of salvation from God is infinitely more precious. But still, receiving this gift requires mental, physical, and spiritual action from us. That is why our linked connection to God the Father is so important. We must actively work on our perspective in all situations. How do we do that?

As we saw, it begins with confession and repentance.

Confession and Repentance

If we confess our sins, he is faithful and
just and will forgive us our sins and
purify us from all unrighteousness.
(1 John 1:9)

As some have pointed out, evil spelled backward is live. If you want to live, turn from evil. Turning away from sin and toward God is what repentance means. The Bible tells us, "Now repent of your sins and turn to God, so that your sins may be wiped away" (Acts 3:19 NLT). Repentance leads to confession.

The Greek word for confession, *homologeó*, means "to agree or come to the same conclusion."[11] When we confess, we agree with God that we have sinned. God promises to forgive our sins and make us holy. As the Apostle John says, "If we confess our sins, he is faithful and just and will forgive us our sins and purify us from all unrighteousness" (1 John 1:9).

We are God's children, connected to Him through His love and Jesus's death and resurrection. He promises never to leave us or forsake us (Deuteronomy 31:8). But that does not mean our lives will be easy. We are in a spiritual battle against sin, evil, and Satan. Satan can't control us, but he can influence and confuse us by using our minds, tempting us, and fueling our fears, uncertainty, or misguided thoughts.

We need to protect and take care of our minds and our bodies. After all, our bodies belong to God: "Don't you realize that your body is the temple of the Holy Spirit, who lives in you and was given to you by God? You do not belong to yourself" (1 Corinthians 6:19 NLT).

Think about the times you had your worst arguments and lost your cool. Most likely, you were tired, hungry, dehydrated, or not feeling well. When our bodies are weak—late at night, after drinking a lot, or during high stress—we often do things we regret later.

The Apostle Paul tells us how to fight spiritual battles: "Put on all of God's armor so that you will be able to stand firm against all strategies of the devil" (Ephesians 6:11 NLT). He reminds us of this:

> For though we live in the world, we do not wage war as the world does. The weapons we fight with are not the weapons of the world. On the contrary, they have divine power to demolish strongholds. We demolish arguments and every pretension that sets itself up against the knowledge of God, and we take captive every thought to make it obedient to Christ. (2 Corinthians 10:3–5)

How do we take every thought captive? James tells us, "Submit yourselves to God. Resist the devil, and he will run away from you" (James 4:7 GNT). The best time to win the battle of your mind is to win the fight before it happens. Take control of your thoughts. Keep feeding your mind the truth. Free your mind from bad thoughts by changing channels. Instead, concentrate on what God wants you to focus on.

Temptation itself isn't a sin. We can't control the thoughts that enter our minds, but we can grab hold of those thoughts before they start to influence our actions. When our thoughts start to arouse our emotions and feelings, it's more difficult to refocus our attention away from that thought. Once we lose control of our emotions and feelings, it's easier to act on the temptation.

Any desire that runs away and controls us becomes wicked and twisted, and will become sinful. If you want to quit a bad habit, you first need to stop paying attention to that habit. In the same way, to stop a sin pattern in your life, you need to refocus your thoughts, time, and energy on something else.

Our minds are constantly filled with thoughts and ideas. Once the train has left the station, it's hard to turn it back around. Start early; be aggressive and intentional about it. You can't fight a feeling or emotion, but you can fight the thought process, and you can fight the attention you pay to that sin. Remember, you don't need to let the birds make their nest in your hair just because they are flying overhead.

Jesus was tempted by everything we're tempted by today. Just because we believe in God and want to follow Jesus doesn't mean we will not be tempted. Satan will tempt us for our entire human lives. The good news is that Satan isn't omniscient. He doesn't know what we're thinking or what we will think about tomorrow or the next day. He's predictable and has used the same tricks on people for thousands of years. We *all* have the same issues and temptations.

> The temptations in your life are no different from what others experience. And God is faithful. He will not allow the temptation to be more than you can stand. When you are tempted, he will show you a way out so that you can endure. (1 Corinthians 10:13 NLT)

You will be tempted, but God promises to give you a way to overcome temptation. He hears us when we pray and will forgive us when we confess our sins and repent.

Forgiveness and Prayer

Since he did not spare even his own
Son but gave him up for us all, won't
he also give us everything else?
(Romans 8:32 NLT)

God knows our true hearts. We can't and shouldn't try to hide our desires or sinful ways from Him. We need to repent and confess so our hearts become empty of sin and God can fill us up with His love, grace, and mercy.

As we receive forgiveness, we can begin to forgive others. Our selfish human condition means that although we want forgiveness from God for our sins, we have a hard time forgiving everyone else's sins.

Don't weaken your connection to God by holding onto pointless, sinful feelings. God forgives us willingly, even many times a day, for all our sins. When we are unwilling to forgive others who hurt us, we undermine the power of the forgiveness we've received. The good news is that God can forgive even the sin of being unforgiving. We just have to turn to Him.

It's sad that many believers feel like God won't or doesn't answer prayers. God will *always* answer your prayers in one of three ways: no, yes, or not yet. God is all-knowing and sovereign. He is a good Father, as Jesus reminded the disciples:

> You parents—if your children ask for a loaf of bread, do you give them a stone instead? Or if they ask for a fish, do you give them a snake? Of course not! So if you sinful people know how to give good gifts to your children, how much more will your

heavenly Father give good gifts to those who ask him. (Matthew 7:9–11 NLT)

God knows what's best for us and sees the big picture, just like we can see the big picture when our children ask for something.

Remember, if you ask and have faith, it will be given to you, if it's for God's glory. We will always need to explore the intentions of our requests. Maybe even our misguided requests can be straightened out and eventually grounded on solid footings when we're patient. Maybe that's when God says, "Not yet" or "Wait a little longer."

In Mark's Gospel, we see that Jesus answers even the demons' requests. When Jesus casts the demons out of the possessed man at Gerasenes, the demons beg Jesus not to torture them. The demons, Legion, ask to be sent into the nearby herd of pigs instead (Mark 5:1–16).

The demons didn't have to keep asking and begging repeatedly. They knew Jesus could either grant their request, deny it, or defer it until later. Jesus granted their request, and that was the end. Think about it. These were evil demons having their request granted. How much more will God do for us?

Jesus reminds us that we are so much more valuable to God: "Are not five sparrows sold for two pennies? Yet not one of them is forgotten by God. Indeed, the very hairs of your head are all numbered. Don't be afraid; you are worth more than many sparrows" (Luke 12:6–7).

God hears our prayers, loves us, forgives us, and promises to care for us. After all, He proved His love by sending Jesus to restore our connection with Him (Romans 8:32). We can join with Paul to praise God: "Thank God! He gives us victory over sin and death through our Lord Jesus Christ" (1 Corinthians 15:57 NLT).

We can trust that God will continue to work in our lives until Jesus returns or we go to heaven to be with him: "I am certain that God, who began the good work within you, will continue his work until it is finally finished on the day when Christ Jesus returns" (Philippians 1:6 NLT).

Knowing that God is at work in us, we can turn our attention to strengthening any weak links we may have. In the next couple of chapters, we will discuss some of the most common sins that damage our connection with God and how to take our thoughts captive in those situations.

Greed and Pride

*There are seven things that the LORD hates and
cannot tolerate: A proud look, a lying tongue,
hands that kill innocent people, a mind that thinks
up wicked plans, feet that hurry off to do evil,
a witness who tells one lie after another, and
someone who stirs up trouble among friends.*
(Proverbs 6:16–19 GNT)

The thoughts in our mind shape our attitude, and our attitude drives our actions. These habits and behaviors define our character, either fortifying the links that bind us to God or weakening them, leaving us vulnerable to spiritual disconnection. The steps we take matter, but the *purpose* behind them is what determines their eternal impact.

Pride. Deceit. Greed. These are not just flaws. They are signals that warn us when we're veering off the path of humility, truth, and love. The question is this: How do we recognize these traits in ourselves and take the necessary steps to break the chains of sin and replace them with a stronger bond to God's will?

Pastor Rick Warren once asked, "Have you ever felt like you are a hostage to your thoughts?"[12] It's a question that cuts deep because so many of us live this reality. Our minds can become traps, replaying the same stories on a loop, stories convincing us of lies that shape our reality.

The more these lies play, the more convincing they become. And once we buy into them, they start shaping everything: our emotions, our actions, and even how we see ourselves. It all begins in the mind.

Think about it. Have you ever been stuck in a loop of thoughts you couldn't escape? Or have you found yourself doing something you know you shouldn't, such as seeking out content you regret, snapping at someone you care about, or falling back into a habit you've tried to break? You know it's wrong, but you do it anyway. Why? Because there's a battle raging inside you.

Paul described this perfectly in Romans 7:23 (GNT): "But I see a different law at work in my body—a law that fights against the law which my mind approves of. It makes me a prisoner to the law of sin which is at work in my body." Paul called it a law at work in our bodies that fights against what we know is right, making us prisoners to sin. This is a full-scale war for your mind and soul, not a fleeting battle. And it's not fought on one front.

Three forces are working against us at all times: our old self, the world, and Satan. That former self, the person you were before Jesus transformed your life, isn't your ally. It clings to what's familiar, replaying old habits and patterns that pull you down. The world feeds us lies, glorifying sin and distorting truth. Satan exploits our weaknesses, whispering doubts and temptations.

You have to realize and remember that you are not powerless. The first step to winning this battle is recognizing it for what it is. Thoughts aren't facts. Just because something pops into your head doesn't make it true. Your mind isn't your enemy, but it does need to be trained.

Spiritual growth comes from learning to separate truth from deception, and that takes effort. It's not automatic. It requires self-control, reflection, and patience. This isn't a one-time fix. It's a daily practice. You must consistently challenge your thoughts throughout the day and for the rest of your life.

The Bible gives us a clear guide: "Those who are dominated by the sinful nature think about sinful things, but those who are controlled by the Holy Spirit think about things that please the Spirit" (Romans 8:5 NLT). This verse is more than a reminder; it's a call to action. It's about intentionally choosing what you focus on and aligning your thoughts with God's truth.

Now let's talk about habits. So much of what we do every day is automatic. From brushing your teeth to checking your phone, these routines are hardwired into your brain. But here's the thing: Those routines can be rewired. You *can* create habits that reflect God's truth instead of the lies you've been believing. It takes time and intention, but it is possible.

Every time you choose to challenge a lie, every time you align your thoughts with God's truth, you're taking ground in this fight. You're stepping into the freedom and victory that God has already promised you. This is a fight worth engaging in, and you already have what it takes to win.

Greed and Generosity

Honor the LORD by making him an
offering from the best of all that your
land produces. If you do, your barns
will be filled with grain, and you will
have too much wine to store it all.
(Proverbs 3:9–10 GNT)

Everything we have—our money, our possessions, even our time—isn't truly ours. It's on loan from God. When you start seeing life through that lens, it shifts your perspective entirely. There are two kinds of people in this world: givers and takers. The Bible emphasizes giving more than it speaks about faith, hope, and love combined. Why? Because generosity is one of the purest ways to express the eternal values of faith, hope, and love.

Greed is an insatiable hunger for more. It's not just about materialism or wanting things. It's about comparison, pride, and control. Greedy people often keep score: "How much do I have compared to my neighbor? How do I measure up?" For some, it's about proving their worth through financial success or chasing status, signaling with cars, jewelry, or other material possessions. But greed is a trap. It's a bottomless pit that can never be satisfied.

The Bible is often misquoted as saying, "Money is the root of all evil." But the verse actually says, "For the *love* of money is a root of *all kinds* of evil" (1 Timothy 6:10, emphasis added).

Loving money is at the root of many sins. God doesn't oppose wealth. He opposes greed.

Jesus even praised the good and faithful servant in His parable of investing. But when money becomes your master, when it's hoarded out of fear or used to inflate your pride, it becomes destructive.

Hoarding often stems from two places: fear and pride. Fear says, "What if I don't have enough?" Pride says, "Look how much I've got." Both lead to a scarcity mindset where trust shifts from God to possessions. People hoard out of fear of losing what they have or pride in showing what they've accumulated.

But this mindset is flawed. The Bible reminds us, "Don't love money; be satisfied with what you have. For God has said, 'I will never fail you. I will never abandon you'" (Hebrews 13:5 NLT). Trusting in God's provision frees us from the chains of fear and pride.

The key difference between hoarding and saving lies in motivation. Hoarding is driven by fear and pride, while saving is an act of stewardship. Saving is about practicing self-control, preparing for the future, and positioning yourself to give generously. Proverbs tell us, "The wise have wealth and luxury, but fools spend whatever they get" (Proverbs 21:20 NLT). Saving isn't about stockpiling out of fear. It's about managing resources wisely.

If you're unsure whether your actions reflect hoarding or wise saving, consider these key principles that define purposeful saving:

- **To Build Discipline**

Saving teaches self-control and helps us resist the pull of instant gratification. It's a spiritual discipline that builds character and strengthens faith.

- **To Let Money Work for You**

  Saving allows you to invest and grow your resources, turning money into a tool rather than a master. In the book of Ecclesiastes, it says, "Invest your money in foreign trade, and one of these days you will make a profit" (Ecclesiastes 11:1 GNT).

- **To Give Generously**

  Saving positions you to bless others. The Old Testament prophet Malachi challenges us to bring our tithes to God, promising that He will "open the windows of heaven" and pour out blessings we can't contain (Malachi 3:10 NLT). Tithing isn't just about money; it's about trust. It's a way to thank God for the past, prioritize Him in the present, and trust Him with the future.

Money is like farm manure in many ways. Money is meant to flow, bless others, and make a true impact. Money should be spread around and used as a tool or resource. Hoarding money is like stacking up fertilizer in a pile. It starts to stink and rot. But when you spread it around, it helps things grow.

God calls us to fairness and integrity in how we earn and use money. Are we treating others fairly? Are we using our talents to serve, or are we taking advantage of others? God blesses businesses and families that put people first—customers, employees, communities—while still making a profit. Success and integrity aren't mutually exclusive; they go hand in hand.

At the end of the day, everything we have is temporary. Jesus said, "And what do you benefit if you gain the whole world but lose your own soul? Is anything worth more than your soul?" (Matthew 16:26 NLT). Riches won't save us on Judgment Day. We can't buy our salvation, but following God's instructions and walking with Jesus can.

We need to stop being people pleasers and start being God pleasers. It's actually a much easier and better way to live. Let me share a story that taught me this lesson in a way I'll never forget.

Living for an Audience of One

Riches will do you no good on the day you
face death, but honesty can save your life.
(Proverbs 11:4 GNT)

It was my twenty-fifth college reunion at Colgate University. My wife and daughter were heading south for a lacrosse tournament, so my son and I drove north to upstate New York. The weather was perfect, rare for that area where you can experience all four seasons in a single day. I had my prepared notes for the speech I was scheduled to give, and I even practiced them out loud with my nine-year-old son during the drive. My wife, who's a fantastic public speaker, had already given me her feedback, so I felt ready.

But somewhere between arriving on campus and having a couple of cocktails with my classmates, I decided to change my opening remarks. I was set to close the main dinner ceremony with some thank-yous and final thoughts. The university president had just delivered a heartfelt speech, and as I hugged him and stepped up to the microphone, I started with "Wow!

Thank you, President. You are amazing. Your words were so touching and moving." So far, so good.

Then I veered off course. I decided to be a people pleaser instead of a God pleaser. I said, "Speaking of amazing, how about all our female classmates in attendance? They look absolutely amazing too." The words themselves weren't terrible, but my delivery was off. I was trying too hard to get laughs and approval. Even the men I was trying to impress started grimacing and waving me off from the back row. The woman I was trying to flatter looked uncomfortable. I sensed the awkwardness and tried to recover by calling out specific women's names to recognize them, but that only made things worse. Faces turned red, and the grimaces multiplied.

I eventually moved on to the rest of my prepared remarks, which were God-centered and focused on gratitude, perspective, and becoming the best version of ourselves. A few people came up to me afterward to say they enjoyed my speech, which made me feel a little better. But many more teased me about my opening remarks and how I had "messed up."

During the four-hour drive home and in the days that followed, I couldn't shake the feeling of being unfulfilled, unsettled, and unsatisfied. I prayed for clarity, and God, through the Holy Spirit, revealed the truth to me. I hadn't been rude or offensive, but I had shifted my focus. Instead of keeping the spotlight on God and using my words to inspire my classmates and maybe even lead them closer to Jesus, I had made it about me. I wanted to impress them, make them laugh, and remind them how "cool" we were twenty-five years ago. My opening remarks had become worldly, common, and uninspiring.

When you live for an audience of One, when you focus on pleasing God, you'll find authentic peace and satisfaction. People's opinions are fleeting, but God's truth is eternal. Most people are confused, opinionated, and constantly changing their minds. God, on the other hand, is constant, true, and everlasting. Every thought He has ever had is the same today, yesterday, and forever. Pleasing Him is not only easier but also far more fulfilling.

That weekend, I recognized where I had fallen short—where I had sinned by seeking approval from people instead of God. I prayed and asked Jesus to help me turn away from those desires and focus on my true audience of One: Jesus. When you live for him, you'll not only inspire and move others as a byproduct but you'll also live a life of peace and satisfaction. Let's aim to play, pray, study, prepare, speak, serve, and live for him. That's what truly pleases God—fortifying the unbreakable links that anchor us to Him, keeping our connection steadfast, pure, and enduring.

Pride and Humility

God is against the proud, but He gives
grace to the humble. So give yourselves
completely to God. . . . Come near to
God, and God will come near to you.
(James 4:6–8 NCV)

Pride is a silent, toxic killer. It's like carbon monoxide: odorless, tasteless, and invisible, yet deadly. It sneaks into your life, often unnoticed, and begins to poison your relationships, your decisions, and your connection with God. At its core, pride is the root of most sins. It's the belief that you don't need God, that you can do it all on your own. And that mindset is dangerous.

How do you know if pride is an issue for you? Start by asking yourself a few questions:

- How do you react when someone offers you advice?
- How do you handle criticism or rejection?
- How important are compliments and praise to you?
- Are you glued to your phone, checking for likes and comments on social media?

These behaviors might seem small, but they can reveal a much deeper issue. Social media, in particular, has amplified pride in our culture. It has created a world where validation comes from likes and comments, shaping our perspective on reality and influencing our thought patterns. This mindset isn't confined to adults; it's shaping the next generation in ways we can't ignore.

Pride is about positioning: status, importance, and self-reliance. It's the mindset of "I'm self-made" or "I did it my way." But if you truly believe that, where does God fit into your life? Pride is one of the main obstacles that keeps people out of heaven. It was the very sin that caused Satan's fall. He wanted to be recognized for his beauty and power—to be God. And for that, he was cast out of heaven like a bolt of lightning.

Pride doesn't just separate us from God; it hardens our hearts to His voice. Jesus told His disciples a parable, saying, "A farmer went out to plant his seed. As he scattered it across his field, some seed fell on a footpath, where it was stepped on, and the birds ate it" (Luke 8:5 NLT). The footpath represents a hardened heart.

When pride compacts the soil of your heart, God's Word can't penetrate. It just sits on the surface, vulnerable to being snatched away by the "birds" of the world.

If you trace the root of most sins, you'll find pride. It's the belief that you know best, that you don't need help, that you can do it all on your own. But pride doesn't just affect you; it impacts everyone around you. It poisons relationships, creates division, and leads to isolation. And the longer pride goes unchecked, the harder it becomes to break free. A hardened heart often requires a painful storm to soften it. The deeper the pride, the stronger the storm needed to break it apart.

The antidote to pride is humility, which begins with surrender. It's about recognizing that you can't do it on your own and turning to Jesus for help. When you seek Jesus, the Holy Spirit gives you the strength, power, and desire to humble yourself. It's not about you; it's about God. It's about serving Him, pleasing Him, and living for His glory.

Becoming humble doesn't mean thinking less of yourself. It means thinking of yourself less. It's about shifting your focus from your desires and ambitions to God's purpose for your life. And when you do that, you'll find freedom, peace, and a deeper connection with Him.

Humility is a daily practice. It's about renewing your mind, taking captive every thought, and aligning your perspective with God's truth. It's about recognizing when pride starts to creep in and choosing to let it go. And it's about remembering that every good thing in your life is a gift from God, not something you earned on your own.

The truth is that pride will always try to sneak back in. But when you stay close to God, when you surrender to Him daily, He will give you the grace and strength to overcome it. As James reminds us, "Come near to God and he will come near to you" (James 4:8).

Let's make it our mission to live with humility, to serve others, and to glorify God in everything we do. Because when we do, we not only overcome pride but we become the people God created us to be.

Breaking Old Habits

We demolish arguments and
every pretension that sets itself
up against the knowledge of God,
and we take captive every thought
to make it obedient to Christ.
(2 Corinthians 10:5)

Experts estimate that over 40 percent of our daily actions are shaped by habits ingrained in our routines.[13] Sit with that truth for a moment. Nearly half of what we do every day happens without deliberate thought. It's not the big, dramatic decisions that decide our future but the small, consistent patterns we maintain daily. For better or for worse, these are the habits that pave our path over time.

Take athletes, for example. Whether they're catching a pass, taking a free throw, or lining up the perfect putt, success won't come from luck. Each win is the result of habits they've practiced over and over again. Those routines are intentionally crafted to create muscle memory and enhance focus, enabling athletes to not only handle the pressure but to thrive in it. It's not random; it's discipline.

In the same way, faith isn't something that just happens. Bold, authentic trust calls us to take action and intentionally renew our focus on Jesus, even in the waiting. It's about aligning our thoughts and actions with God's truth rather than our own distorted view. When you realize that habits drive nearly half of your daily actions, you can't doubt the significance of shaping those patterns to reflect a God-honoring life.

Renewing your mind doesn't have to feel overwhelming if you start small. Identify one of two recurring thoughts that weaken your link to God and challenge them. Talk back to the voice that whispers, "I am alone," and replace it with the truth: "I am called and cared for by the Creator of the universe."[14]

Constantly remind yourself of God's oath to never leave or forsake you. There are over 7,000 promises in the Bible about His love, protection, mercy, and grace.[15] When you accept those truths as your guide, you'll step into the life God designed for you with clarity, purpose, and alignment.

Our connection to God starts in the heart. We need to ask Jesus to save us from our sinful nature. That's why He came, suffered, died, and rose again for us. Once we've had this spiritual heart transplant, we can begin to focus on renewing our minds. But here's the key: It starts with changing the way we think about everything.

Many of us were taught that our brains are fully developed by age ten and that "we are who we are." That's simply not true. Neuroscience now confirms what the Bible has said for thousands of years: We are constantly learning, growing, and changing.[16] Through our thoughts, we can reshape our behavior, actions, and character.

Unlike animals, we were created with the unique ability to communicate with God and control our thoughts. The Bible reminds us, "The human heart is the most deceitful of all things, and desperately wicked. Who really knows how bad it is? But I, the LORD, search all hearts and examine secret motives" (Jeremiah 17:9–10 NLT). That is why we can't trust our hearts or gut feelings. They're often influenced by lies and worldly experiences. Instead, we must focus on controlling our minds.

Here's the chain reaction:

Control your mind, and you can control your thoughts.

Control your thoughts, and you can control your perspective.

Control your perspective, and you can control your attitude.

Control your attitude, and you can control your behavior and actions.

Control your actions, and you develop the character that God desires.

This process begins with mind control. Highly enlightened and spiritually mature people can focus their minds throughout the day, but most of us get busy, tired, and distracted. We let our emotions dictate our behavior, missing the process God wants us to follow. That is what weakens our connection to Him.

The key to strengthening your relationship with God is simple: Recognize the chains that bind you and admit your inability to break them on your own. Ask Jesus for his supernatural power to set you free and alert you whenever a feeling or emotion triggers something in you. God created us with emotions, and they're not inherently bad. But they can serve as alarms, signaling when we need to pause and reflect on His truth.

If you're tempted by materialism, recall what God says about greed. If you're drawn to someone who isn't your spouse, let God's Word remind you of the dangers of lust and adultery. If someone wrongs you, let your pride and ego take a back seat as you reflect on God's call for humility, mercy, and grace.

The media often glorifies sin, showing only the excitement of forbidden actions while ignoring the pain, betrayal, and brokenness they cause. But God's Word offers a better way—a way that leads to peace, fulfillment, and eternal joy.

Breaking old habits and building new ones is achievable with God's support. Start small. Focus on renewing your mind daily. Recognize the lies you've been believing and replace them with God's truth. Remember that progress, not perfection, is what moves you closer to God's truth. As you take those steps, you'll find your connection to God growing stronger, your character becoming more like Christ, and your life reflecting His glory.

Every feeling and emotion we experience has a purpose. While we often focus on overcoming negative emotions, let's not overlook the incredible, God-given emotions that bring joy and connection. Those moments are gifts meant to remind us of His goodness and draw us closer to Him.

Think about the warmth of a hug, the intimacy with your spouse, or the awe of standing on a beach or hiking a mountain. Those feelings are intentional blessings designed to reflect God's love and creativity. Our senses—touch, taste, sight, hearing—allow us to experience His creation in ways that should trigger gratitude and praise. Every sunset, every laugh, every moment of wonder is an opportunity to thank Him for His goodness.

Don't lose sight of the good as you work to break old habits. Celebrate the positive moments that remind you of God's presence and love. Gratitude for those blessings will not only deepen your connection to Him but also help you build habits rooted in His truth. Every perfect gift, including the ability to feel joy, is from above. Let's make it a daily practice to praise Him for it.

Pride, greed, and the battle for our thoughts are all part of the same fight, a fight for our hearts and minds. But God has already equipped us with the tools to win. Today, choose humility over pride, generosity over greed, and truth over lies. Take one step closer to the life He's calling you to live.

As we reflect on the dangers of pride and greed, it's clear that those sins don't stand alone. They give rise to others, shaping how we see ourselves, our possessions, and our purpose. In the next chapter, we'll cover how pride fuels those sins and distorts our connection to God.

Envy, Lust, Anger, and Selfishness

For if you live according to your human nature,
you are going to die; but if by the Spirit you put to
death your sinful actions, you will live.
(Romans 8:13 GNT)

Every day we face choices that either bring us closer to God or pull us away from Him. Envy, lust, anger, and selfishness can quietly take root in our hearts, creating barriers that weaken the links in our connection to Him. Those emotions often go unnoticed at first, but over time, they distort our thoughts, cloud our judgment, and disrupt our peace.

Think of the links connecting you to God. Each represents love, trust, faith, and obedience. When envy creeps in, it weakens the connection. Lust shifts your focus, anger builds walls, and selfishness creates distance. Those forces don't just affect your relationship with God. They ripple through every part of your life, creating confusion and chaos where there should be clarity and peace.

Many Christians often wonder why they feel unfulfilled and unsatisfied. It's because their connection to God is just as weak as that of nonbelievers. But no matter how far those emotions have taken you, God offers a way back. Through His Word, He provides the tools to confront those struggles and strengthen weakened links to Him. This chapter is about recognizing the cracks, understanding their impact, and taking intentional steps to restore your connection with God. Progress starts with awareness, and freedom comes through action.

Envy is one of the most subtle yet destructive forces that can take root in our hearts. It's not just a fleeting feeling but a mindset that grows quietly, creating cracks in the chain that connects us to the Lord. It's like rust, silently eating away at the links of love, trust, faith, and obedience until they snap.

The unavoidable sinful nature of envy— the desire for something that belongs to someone else—doesn't necessarily sever our connection to God at first. But when envy takes root and bitterness starts to grow, that's when it becomes fatal. You begin to lose sight of God's call as the hollowing bitterness whispers, "Why not *me*?"

Envy creates chaos in our lives far greater than we realize. It clouds our judgment, poisons our relationships, and distances us from God. As the universal thief of peace and joy, envy reminds you of what you lack and robs the beauty of what you already have.

One of the deadliest characteristics of envy is its piercing silence. Rather than announcing itself, it sneaks in as a quiet destroyer, taking root and eroding the foundation of our connection with God.

Envy is like a boomerang; it always comes back. And when it does, it hits *hard*. It never actually harms the person you are envious of, but it absolutely destroys you. You may think you are sending it out to hurt someone else, but when the wind shifts, it's coming straight for you.

No matter how far or fast you throw it, no matter how hard you try to aim it elsewhere, it finds its way back to you at speeds you can't even imagine. It doesn't just graze you; it smacks you right in the face, leaving you dazed and wondering how the heck you got there.

Allowing resentment to linger in your heart creates a stubborn wedge between you and Jesus. That barrier innately weakens your connection to God. He's still there, steady and constant, but you're so consumed by what you don't have that you miss what He's trying to hand you. Envy clouds your vision, muffles God's voice, and numbs your ability to experience His presence.

When envy takes root, it refuses to sit quietly in the background; it grows, festers, and starts to secretly shape your perspective. It's like a filter over your eyes, distorting everything you look at. Instead of seeing opportunity, you see lack. Rather than feeling joy for others, you harbor resentment.

And here's the thing: Envy doesn't always show up in big, obvious ways. It often seeps in through thin cracks like when you're scrolling on social media and feel that little twitch of

"Why not me?" or you hear about someone else's success and immediately compare it to your own.

This is exactly where and why the boomerang effect becomes so lethal. The more you allow envy to linger, the more it comes back to you, magnifying those potent feelings of inadequacy and dissatisfaction. You're left trapped in a vicious cycle that can only be broken by recognizing it for what it is: a distraction from the devil.

The Comparison Trap

Do not let your heart envy sinners, but
always be zealous for the fear of the Lord.
(Proverbs 23:17)

So what is envy *really* about? Does it actually matter in the grand scheme of things? The Bible clearly tells us that "God created mankind in His own image" (Genesis 1:27). We are His masterpiece, uniquely crafted with love and intention. So when we view someone else's physical appearance, material possessions, and earthly successes with envy, we're essentially telling God, "You messed up with me."

Think about that for a second. We are telling the Creator of the universe, the Alpha and the Omega, the One who designed us with infinite care, that His work is somehow flawed. That's pretty arrogant, right? It's like a beautiful clay pot looking at the master potter and saying, "You got it wrong."

The rest of creation seems to understand this. Imagine if one bird species envied another for its feathers, or if one animal resented another for having more legs. Does the horse look at the giraffe and envy its neck length? It sounds absurd, doesn't it? Yet as humans, we fall into this trap all too often.

Comparison is one of the sneakiest traps we fall into. It's subtle, but it's powerful. It can take a good day and turn it sour in an instant. And the truth is, when we compare ourselves to others, only two things can happen. We either feel superior or we feel inferior. Neither of those outcomes strengthens our link to God. In fact, both weaken it.

We often use the terms *jealousy* and *envy* interchangeably, defining them as the desire for someone else's blessings. However, the truth is that they are distinct emotions with very different impacts on our hearts and minds.

Jealousy often stems from a fear of losing something we value, saying, "I'm sad I don't have it." On the other hand, envy takes it a step further, saying, "I'm angry that you have it."

Here's the key difference: Jealousy is protective—rooted in longing or insecurity about what we have or wish to have. Envy, however, is corrosive. It doesn't just want what someone else has; it resents them for having it. Envy doesn't stop at wanting; it seeks to diminish the other person's joy.

Picture jealousy as a seed and envy as the vine it grows into when left unchecked. Jealousy might start as a fleeting feeling, but if we don't confront it, it can twist into a destructive force that poisons our hearts and relationships.

This distinction matters because envy is far more dangerous to our spiritual and emotional well-being. It distorts our perspectives to see others' blessings as a source of bitterness rather than a testament of God's goodness. It convinces us that

God's blessings are limited, that someone else's gain must equate to our loss.

Many people don't recognize comparison as a thief. It robs you of your joy, peace, and ability to see the blessings in your own life. It's like carrying around a thousand-pound weight while trying to run a race—you're not going to get very far. And the worst part? It's a trap we set for ourselves.

When you compare your life to someone else's, you're only seeing the highlight reel. You don't see the struggles behind the scenes. That person with the perfect house? They might be drowning in debt. The one with the dream job? They could be battling loneliness. The truth is, you never know what someone else is going through. So why waste your energy comparing your reality to their illusion?

The Bible warns us not to get caught up in what others have or what they're doing. Proverbs warns, "Do not let your heart envy sinners, but always be zealous for the fear of the LORD" (Proverbs 23:17). Focus on your relationship with God. That's where true fulfillment comes from.

Instead of comparing yourself to those around you, compare yourself to Jesus. Are you growing more like him? Are you becoming more aligned with God's will? That's the only comparison that matters. When you see someone else succeeding, don't let envy creep in. Instead, use their success as proof of what's possible. Celebrate them, pray for them, and then get back to focusing on your own journey.

Remember, God is constant. He never pulls away from us; we are the ones who drift. Comparison is one of the ways we fall away, but it doesn't have to be. When you shift your focus from others to God, you'll find the peace and joy you've been searching for.

Envy and Redemption

Create a pure heart in me, O God, and
renew a steadfast spirit within me.
(Psalm 51:10)

Throughout the Bible, envy is revealed as a deeply ingrained part of human nature—a twisted spirit that has resided in us since the fall of mankind. It doesn't need justification to surface; it simply exists, waiting for the perfect opportunity to pounce. Time and again, we see how envy leads to destruction, yet God's grace transforms even the darkest moments into something good.

I'm sure you've heard the story of Cain and Abel. Cain murdered his brother out of envy because Abel found favor with God. It wasn't about fairness or justice; it was envy, plain and simple, that drove Cain to commit the first murder in history.

Then there's Joseph whose brothers were so consumed by envy over their father's love for him that they sold him into slavery. But one of the most powerful examples of envy and redemption is found in the life of Stephen and Saul of Tarsus. Stephen, a faithful disciple of Jesus, was performing miracles and leading many to follow Christ. His faith and influence stirred up resentment among the religious leaders who falsely accused him and ultimately stoned him to death.

Acts 6 and 7 document Stephen's final moments. As he was being stoned, he saw the heavens open to reveal Jesus standing at the right hand of God's throne. Stephen was welcomed into heaven with a gesture of love, honor, and respect from the King of kings. Even in Stephen's suffering, his faith never wavered. His very last breaths were used to lift himself up without tearing his enemies down, mirroring Jesus's selflessness on the cross: "Lord, do not hold this sin against them" (Acts 7:60).

Here's where the story takes an interesting turn. Among the crowd witnessing Stephen's death was a young Jewish man named Saul of Tarsus. Saul was a zealous persecutor of Christians, consumed by hatred and determined to destroy the early church. Acts 7:58 tells us that Saul approved of Stephen's stoning, standing by as the first Christian martyr was killed.

While the Bible doesn't explicitly say this moment began Saul's transformation, it's hard to imagine that Stephen's unwavering faith and final prayer, "Lord, do not hold this sin against them," didn't leave an impression. Perhaps it planted a seed in Saul's heart, one that would later bloom on the road to Damascus where he encountered Jesus and was forever changed. Saul became Paul, the man who would write much of the New Testament, establish churches, and lead countless souls to Christ.

It is natural to wonder why Stephen had to suffer and die in such a brutal, public manner. Why do bad things happen to good people? How can a God of love be so cruel? But this story reminds us that God can use even the most evil and senseless acts for good. Stephen's death was far from the conclusion of the story; it was the beginning of Saul's powerful transformation into Paul, whose life and work would change the course of history.

This is the beauty of God's omnipotent grace. He molds what was made for harm into breathtaking works of redemption. Envy may lead to destruction, but destruction is never the end of the story when God is the author. And thankfully, God always holds the pen. His love and power can redeem dark moments, tortured souls, and broken links. When we trust Him, we discover insurmountable peace and purpose, even in the midst of suffering.

Envy weakens the links in the chain that connect you to God, but you don't have to live with it anymore. You can repair weakened links and even strengthen them so they don't crack again. Breaking free from envy isn't about trying to force you to stop comparing or burying those feelings deep down. Let's be real. That's not a battle we're qualified to win on our own.

We must allow God to do the heavy lifting, transforming our hearts and redirecting our focus. When you surrender to Him, you'll find freedom, clarity, and peace in His plan. Here are some practical steps to help you get there:

- **Recognize and Name Your Envy**

   The first step to repairing your chain is to admit where it's weak. Be honest with yourself. Make a list of the people or things you're envious of. Is it someone's success, their appearance, or their possessions? Write it all down. Then ask yourself, "Why do I desire those things?" This isn't about judgment; it's about clarity. When you name your envy, you take away its power to hide in the shadows.

- **Offer It All to God**

   Once you've identified your envy, bring it to God. Confess those desires openly and ask for His forgiveness. This isn't just about saying you're sorry; it's about surrendering. Admit that you can't overcome envy on your own and ask for God's supernatural help. As the Bible reminds us, "I will give you a new heart and put a new spirit in you; I will remove from you your heart of stone and give you a heart of flesh" (Ezekiel 36:26). This is the heart transplant we all need—a transformation that only God can provide.

- **Delight in God, Not the World**

When your heart is made new, you'll find that God's love fills the spaces envy once occupied. Paul reminds us, "If God is for us, who can be against us?" (Romans 8:31). Everything in this world is temporary—possessions, status, even the things we envy. But God's love is eternal. When you delight in Him, you'll discover a peace and joy that no material thing can provide.

- **Remember Your Role as a Steward**

Everything we have is on loan from God. We're not owners; we're stewards. This perspective shifts your focus from what you lack to what you've been entrusted with. Instead of envying what others have, ask yourself, "How can I honor God with what He's given me?"

- **Fight Envy with God's Promises**

The Bible gives us clear guidance on how to combat envy: "Do not fret because of those who are evil or be envious of those who do wrong, for like the grass they will soon wither, like green plants they will soon die away. Trust in the LORD and do good; dwell in the land and enjoy safe pastures. Take delight in the LORD, and he will give you the desires of your heart" (Psalm 37:1–4).

You can break free from envy's tight grip and step into a life of peace, joy, and deeper connection with God. This is your time to let go of what's holding you back and embrace the blessings that are already yours.

Lust: The Silent Saboteur

*Everything that belongs to the world—
what the sinful self desires, what
people see and want, and everything
in this world that people are so proud
of—none of this comes from the
Father; it all comes from the world.
(1 John 2:16 GNT)*

There's yet another craving born from misplaced desires that leaves us chasing illusions that will never truly fulfill us: lust. It's one of those topics that can make people uncomfortable. It's a silent saboteur that snakes into our lives and wreaks havoc if we let it. And while it's easy to think of lust as being solely about sex, it's so much more than that.

Lust is a constant craving for pleasure, an insatiable hunger for more, whether it's possessions, status, physical beauty, or sexual gratification. It's rooted in hedonism—the pursuit of self-indulgence—and it's one of the most effective ways the enemy weakens and breaks our link to God.

Sexual lust is a topic I've wrestled with personally. Many people think about sex often. Let's not forget that God created sex and physical attraction between a man and a woman as part of His good creation. In fact, I wouldn't be writing this and you wouldn't be reading it if this weren't true. Attraction isn't the issue.

The problem arises when those desires take over, when they start to control our thoughts, emotions, and actions, pulling us away from God's design for intimacy. Rather than serving as a link in the chain connecting us to God, it's the crack that causes the metal to snap.

The Bible is full of stories about sex—some that honor God's plan and others that don't. Those who think the Bible is prudish or anti-sex clearly haven't read it closely. From the beginning with Adam and Eve, we see that God created sex as a gift. He blessed men and women with this beautiful, intimate connection to share as husband and wife.

Now, picture this: Adam's in the Garden of Eden, surrounded by waterfalls, lush greenery, and animals that look like they came straight out of a Disney movie. He's probably thinking, *"This is amazing, but something's missing,"* and then boom!—God introduces Eve. Adam describes her in awe as "bone taken from my bone, and flesh from my flesh" (Genesis 2:23 GNT). That would translate today as "Wow! She's perfect." You can almost hear the "Hallelujah Chorus" in the background. It's a moment of pure wonder, love, and probably a little awkward excitement.

But then, of course, comes the fall. Cue the record scratch. Humanity steps outside of God's will, and that perfect connection starts to weaken. That's where the chain begins to break. They are no longer safe in their perfect world getting lost in each other's eyes as the birds sang and creation itself seemed to celebrate their union. They're just naked—vulnerable and ashamed.

What was meant to be a sacred and beautiful gift became twisted. Lust crept in, turning something God designed for intimacy into something selfish and destructive. It's not just about the act itself; it's about what it does to our hearts, our minds, and our relationships.

Lust becomes a problem when it starts to consume us. When we allow our thoughts, feelings, and actions to be dictated by what the world says about sex—through TV, Hollywood, and pornography—we're stepping outside of God's design. The world glamorizes affairs, casual hookups, and forbidden desires, making them seem exciting and romantic. But in reality, they lead to broken hearts, shattered families, and a weakened connection with God.

Many people justify their struggles with lust by saying, "This is just how I am." But that's a lie. You weren't born that way. Somewhere along the line, you started consuming more and more photos, movies, porn, and fantasies, and they began to consume you. Lust is an addiction, and like any addiction, it's hard to break. It builds walls between you and your loved ones, and most importantly, it creates a barrier between you and God.

Let's be painfully real for a moment. If you're bringing porn into your home, why would you expect God to bless your family? If you're watching explicit content at work, why would you expect God to bless your business? Living a double life where you indulge in sin one moment and ask for God's blessing the next is hypocrisy.

Let's not sugarcoat it. The porn industry is built on exploitation. Think about the people you're watching. They were once children with dreams of the future. They did not grow up wanting to be porn stars. As Christians with a link to God and His love, we're better than this. We shouldn't be sponsoring an industry that destroys lives.

Lust isn't just a bad habit; it's an addiction. And like any addiction, it doesn't just go away on its own. It starts small, maybe with a glance or a thought, but over time it grows, consuming your desires, your emotions, and your actions. But here's the thing: Addiction thrives in shame. The more you hide it, the more power it has over you. So instead of beating yourself up or staying stuck in guilt, it's time to shift your focus. What if you could take that same energy, that same drive, and redirect it toward something that builds you up instead of tears you down?

Breaking Free from Lust

For if you live according to your
human nature, you are going to die;
but if by the Spirit you put to death
your sinful actions, you will live.
(Romans 8:13 GNT)

Like any other addiction, lust starts small, grows quietly, and ends up in control before you know it. But you are not powerless. You don't have to stay stuck in this cycle. Jesus lived a human life. He knows what it's like to face temptation. God created us with desires but also gave us the resilience to control them. Lust doesn't define you, and it doesn't have to determine your future. You can break free and strengthen your weakened links with intentional effort and God's help. Let's dive into the steps to reclaim your heart, mind, and soul.

- **Recognize the Problem**

  The first step is admitting that lust is not a harmless, private indulgence; it's an addiction that damages your relationships, your peace, and your connection with God. Living a double-minded life—asking for God's blessings while feeding an addiction—is the definition of hypocrisy. Recognizing this is the first step toward change.

- **Understand Temptation**

  Temptation itself is not a sin; it's what you do with it that matters. Temptation follows a process: Attention (something hooks your mind), Arousal (your emotions kick in), and Action (you act on those feelings). The key is to stop the process at the very beginning. When you feel tempted, pause and take control of your thoughts. Remember, your mind controls your emotions, and your emotions control your actions. As the Bible says, "We take every thought captive and make it obey Christ" (2 Corinthians 10:5 GNT). The moment you're tempted, stop and redirect your focus.

- **Plan Ahead to Avoid Triggers**

  Pastor Rick Warren gives powerful advice: Don't wait until you're in the back seat of a car with your hormones raging to decide not to fool around. Plan ahead. Identify your triggers—when, where, and how you're most vulnerable—and avoid those situations. If you know certain websites, apps, or even people lead you down the wrong path, cut them out.[17] The Bible tells us, "Plan carefully what you do, and whatever you do will turn out right. Avoid evil and walk straight ahead. Don't go one step off the right way" (Proverbs 4:26–27 GNT). Be proactive, not reactive.

- **Guard Your Heart**

  Your heart can deceive you. It's not enough to rely on good intentions or "trust your gut." Your heart might tell you to leave your spouse for someone else or justify harmful behaviors, but that's not God's plan for you. The Bible reminds us, "Keep your heart above all vigilance, for from it flow the springs of life" (Proverbs 4:23 ESV). Protect your heart by staying grounded in God's Word and surrounding yourself with people who hold you accountable.

- **Pray in the Moment of Temptation**

  When temptation strikes, pray immediately. Ask God for strength and focus your attention on Jesus. God tells us, "Call upon Me in the day of trouble; I shall rescue you, and you will honor Me" (Psalm 50:15 NASB1995). Use your emotions as alarms. When you feel tempted, let it be a signal to run, change the channel, or redirect your energy. Remember, Jesus paid the ultimate price so you could break free from sin.

- **Replace the Habit with Positive Actions**

  When you feel tempted, don't just resist—replace. Turn off the TV, go for a run, hit the gym, read a book, or listen to a sermon or podcast. Redirect your energy into something that builds you up instead of tears you down.

The goal is not just to stop lust but to fill your life with purpose and strengthen your connection to God.

- **Break the Lies and Excuses**

  Every excuse you make to justify lust is a lie. Stop believing the lies and stop lying to yourself. Think about the bigger picture—would you want your loved ones to be exploited in the way the porn industry exploits people? Every time you indulge, you're sponsoring that industry. It's time to close this chapter of your life and move forward.

Breaking free from lust is not easy, but it is possible. Many people have done it, and so can you. I've been there. I spent years trapped in this cycle, and it hurt my relationships, my peace, and my link with God. But when I sought God's help, everything changed. You don't have to fight this battle alone. Jesus is ready to help you break the cycle and step into the life you were meant to live. The question is this: Are you ready to take the first step?

Anger and Forgiveness: The Battle for Peace

If you become angry, do not let
your anger lead you into sin, and
do not stay angry all day.
(Ephesians 4:26 GNT)

Anger, bitterness, and cynicism may seem like separate emotions, but they often share the same root. Anger is the immediate reaction, bitterness is the long-term poison, and cynicism becomes the lens through which you view the world. But what causes those feelings to take hold? Why do people lose their temper at a stranger in traffic or carry resentment for years over past experiences? Why do some believe life is stacked against them, becoming so cynical that they expect the worst from everyone?

It often starts with a misinterpretation—a belief that others are out to get you or that life is unfair. For many, this belief comes from real pain. Maybe a spouse walked out, financial struggles piled up, health challenges hit hard, or the unthinkable happened, such as losing a loved one. Life can feel like a sledgehammer, and when it strikes, you're left with a choice: get bitter or get better.

Bitterness spreads. It eats away at your peace, your health, and your relationships. It's like a toxic cancer that grows from the inside out, weakening the links connecting you to God. And most of the time, the person you're angry with doesn't even know it. They're living their life completely unaware while you're carrying the weight of that anger. You're the one suffering, and it's making you miserable to be around those who are closest to you.

Anger and bitterness ripple out, affecting everyone in your orbit, but you don't have to stay stuck. You have the power to choose a different path. You can let go of the anger, release the bitterness, and start the process of forgiveness. It's not easy, but it's worth it.

Jesus's teachings on anger challenge us to rise above our natural instincts and respond with grace, mercy, and compassion. He teaches us to break the cycle of retaliation and respond in a way that reflects God's mercy. It's not about being weak or passive but about showing strength through restraint. The Bible often speaks of meekness as some of the most desired qualities and characteristics of the most prominent figures in the Bible. Meekness is strength under control.

When someone hurts or offends you, it's rarely about you personally. Often their actions stem from their own pain and struggles. Jesus asks us to look beyond the offense to see the person hiding behind it. Paul reinforces this idea, declaring, "Do not be overcome by evil, but overcome evil with good (Romans 12:21 NIV). Rather than seeking revenge, we are called to trust God to handle justice. Our role is to respond with kindness and compassion, even to those who hurt us. That doesn't mean ignoring or allowing wrongdoing, but it doesn't mean refusing to let anger write the story.

Jesus taught and lived out the principle of turning the other cheek while also standing firm in truth and righteousness. When the Pharisees tried to trap Him with their questions, He responded with wisdom and authority, never backing down from what was right. When He cleared the temple of money changers, He balanced grace with strength, mercy with conviction. He calls us to do the same—to seek peace and show compassion but never at the expense of truth and integrity. Rather than simply avoiding conflict, we must address it with love, wisdom, and courage.

At the heart of anger and conflict often lies our own ego. It's that voice inside that says, "How dare they say that to me?" or "Who do they think they are?" When our ego flares up, it triggers our primal instincts, our fight-or-flight response. Our pulse quickens, our heart races, and our rational thinking shuts down. That is the primitive brain at work, the part designed to protect us from immediate threats. But when the neocortex—the rational, problem-solving part of our brain—is engaged, the primitive brain is quieted.[18] That's when we can pause, reflect, and respond thoughtfully instead of reacting impulsively.

Jesus calls us to take this a step further. When someone cuts you off in traffic or lashes out at you, He says to let it go, and even more, to pray for them. Pray for their safety, their peace, and their healing. You have no idea what they might be going through. Maybe they're rushing to the hospital to say goodbye to a loved one. Maybe they're carrying a burden you can't see. Even if they're just being reckless or rude, that behavior isn't sustainable; it will catch up with them eventually. But it's not our job to teach them a lesson. God didn't create us to judge and police each other. He calls us to show mercy, forgiveness, and gratitude for the gift of life.

Remember, hurt people hurt people. Those who are hurting—physically, emotionally, or spiritually—often lash out at others, sometimes intentionally but more often unintentionally. Our role as Christians is to look beyond their actions and try to understand their pain.

Jesus's teachings challenge us to rise above our instincts and reflect God's love in our actions. By letting go of anger, showing mercy, and seeking peace, we not only heal our relationships but also strengthen our connection with God. Wise people listen more than they speak. They know the difference between words and feelings. When someone says something hurtful, pause, take a deep breath, and ask yourself, "What are they feeling right now to say that?" These are the marks of true wisdom—compassion and consideration in all circumstances. Try focusing on their feelings and not their hurtful words. It takes a tremendously strong, meekfully self-controlled, mature person to do that while it's happening to them. Imagine if more of us did that in practice when we're offended.

Holding onto bitterness creates noise and disharmony in our lives, blocking out our ability to hear God's voice and weakening our links to Him. Jesus's teachings on anger are a call to rise above our sinful reactions and reflect love in every action. We can heal our relationships and strengthen our connection with God by showing mercy and seeking peace. This is the only path to true freedom.

Selfishness and Self-Centered Behavior

Don't do anything from selfish ambition
or from a cheap desire to boast, but be
humble toward one another, always
considering others better than yourselves.
(Philippians 2:3 GNT)

Most of us have a control issue. We feel like we should be in charge of everything, and when something goes wrong, we jump into survival mode. That's our primitive brain kicking in, the part designed to fight for survival. But most of our conflicts aren't life-and-death situations. Yet we react as if they are, and that usually gets us into more trouble.

The Bible gives us a better way. It's clear about how to manage conflicts: slow down, stop reacting out of instinct, and start using the neocortex—the part of the brain that helps us plan, process, and manage conflict. The truth is that most of us didn't take conflict management classes in school, but God's Word is the ultimate guide. Romans 12:17–18 reminds us to live at peace with everyone as far as possible. That means taking responsibility for our part in the conflict and choosing peace over pride.

Unresolved conflict doesn't just mess with your relationships; it weakens your connection with God. Think about it: You can't be yelling at your spouse, disrespecting your family, or holding grudges against a coworker and then expect God to bless your prayers in other areas of your life. Conflict creates noise that drowns out your fellowship with God. If you're living in disharmony with others, it's like breaking the links between you and Him.

Here's a perspective shift that can help when life throws its worst at you. This is earth, not heaven. Earth is messy. It's full of pain, suffering, and injustice. If it weren't, there'd be no need for heaven. Pastor Tim Keller's book *Walking with God Through Pain and Suffering* dives deep into this, but the simple truth is this: We live in a broken world.[19]

When tragedy strikes, like a drunk driver killing an innocent pedestrian, people often blame God. But let's be clear. God didn't make that man drink, get behind the wheel, and cause that tragedy. That was his choice, his free will. God gave us free will so we could choose to love Him, but with that freedom comes the ability to make bad choices.

If God stepped in to prevent every accident, every illness, and every tragedy, then earth would be heaven. There'd be no pain, no death, and no need for a Savior. But that's not the world we live in. God allows us to experience struggles and hardships so we recognize our need for Him. It's through those challenges that many people are drawn to Jesus, our one and only Savior.

The pain and suffering of this world remind us that we're not meant to live for ourselves. We're called to live for God, love others, and help those in need. That's the purpose of this life—to seek God, to love Him, and to reflect His love to the world.

Most of us spend a lot of time thinking about ourselves. It's human nature. We're wired to focus on how decisions will impact our lives, our success, and our happiness. But here's a truth I've spent my whole life learning: Life isn't about me; it's about something so much bigger.

When we're consumed by self-centeredness, we lose sight of God's plan for us. Our perspective becomes narrow, and we start measuring success by worldly standards—money, popularity, possessions. But the Bible calls us to a different standard. God doesn't want us to think less about ourselves. He just wants us to think about ourselves less and more about those around us.

Think about the parable of the seed sower in Luke 8. The seed that fell among thorns represents a preoccupied mind—one that's choked by life's worries, riches, and pleasures. If we're too busy chasing the world's version of success, we'll miss out on the wisdom and clarity God wants to give us. It's like weeds in a garden; they grow when we neglect the soil. The same goes for our spiritual life. If we don't tend to it daily through prayer, Scripture, and reflection, distractions will take over, and our link with God will weaken.

Many of us struggle to make decisions, especially when the stakes feel high. We overthink, overanalyze, and let fear paralyze us. Why? Because we're so focused on ourselves—how the decision will affect our lives, our success, and our happiness. But here's the truth: Life isn't about you; it's about something so much bigger.

I heard Timothy Keller say one time so simply, "Make the decision and you'll know if it was the right one."[20] That's it. No overcomplication, no endless deliberation. Just take the step, and trust that clarity will come through action. This mindset shifts the focus from self-centered fear to faith-driven courage. It's not about perfection; it's about trusting God's plan and moving forward. Make wise plans and do your due diligence. Bring your dreams into the light, put them into God's hands, and Jesus will be a light at your feet, step by step.

When we shift our focus from ourselves to God, everything changes. Our perspective becomes eternal. Instead of comparing ourselves to others, we start seeing life from God's point of view. Pastor Rich Wilkerson Jr. gives an illustration about jumping to the moon, which is a perfect example. After comparing how high he can jump—grabbing the bottom of the basketball net with Lebron James reaching the top of the backboard—Wilkerson goes on to tell us that from our perspective, Lebron James's reach is impressive. But if we change our viewpoint and how we measure, we change our perspective. No matter how high someone can jump on earth, no one can reach the moon.[21]

When you change the perspective, the "little" things don't seem so big or important. Our worldly achievements are insignificant from God's perspective, no matter how impressive they seem to us. What matters is how we live for Him, how we love others, and how we fulfill the purpose He's given us.

The more we focus on Jesus, the sharper our vision becomes. We start to see people, situations, and even ourselves through God's eyes. That's when true wisdom begins to take root, and our broken and weakened links are repaired.

Restoring the Broken Links

I will give you a new heart and a new
mind. I will take away your stubborn heart
of stone and give you an obedient heart.
(Ezekiel 36:26 GNT)

When we live for ourselves, we weaken the links that connect us to God through our pride, selfishness, and fear. These sins keep us from experiencing the fullness of life that God has for us. But here's the good news: God is in the business of restoration.

Ezekiel 36:26 is a powerful promise. God doesn't just want to fix the broken pieces of our lives; He wants to give us a completely new heart and mind. He wants to replace our stubbornness with obedience, our fear with faith, and our self-centeredness with a servant's heart.

Restoring the broken links starts with surrender. It's about admitting that we can't do it on our own and asking God for His supernatural power. It's about making Him the center of our lives—our marriages, our careers, our families. When God is at the center, everything else falls into place.

Think about the statistics on marriage. Couples who pray, read the Bible, and attend church together have a much lower divorce rate than the general public.[22] That's not a coincidence. When God is the foundation of your relationship, it becomes unshakable. The same principle applies to every area of life. If God isn't at the center, the link to Him will break, and everything else will start to unravel.

The media loves sharing that divorce rates are nearly 50 percent. What they rarely tell us is that when one spouse has even a high school education, the divorce rate drops greatly. When a college education is in the marriage, the divorce rate drops precipitously. Pastor Rick Warren has a different perspective. He teaches that if the married couple puts God first in their lives and marriages, attends church weekly, prays together and with fellow community members, the divorce rate is less than 1 percent.[23] *That* is the data that needs to be spread.

So how do we restore the broken links?

- **Make God the Priority**

  Start each day with prayer and Scripture. Invite God into every decision, every challenge, and every moment.

- **Cultivate Humility**

  Let go of selfish ambition and focus on serving others. True greatness comes from putting others first.

- **Stay Connected**

  Surround yourself with a community of believers who will encourage you, challenge you, and help you grow in your faith. Just as Proverbs 27:17 declares, "As iron sharpens iron, so one person sharpens another."

- **Trust the Process**

  Restoration takes time. Be patient and trust that God is working in you to strengthen and repair your weak and broken links, even when you can't see it.

When we let God take the lead, He transforms our hearts, our minds, and our lives. He restores our broken links that separate us from Him and sets us free to live with purpose, passion, and peace.

Repairing
Broken Links

I'll never forget hearing Andy Stanley speak at Saddleback Church in California. In addressing nonbelievers, he expressed something that struck me deeply: "Even if you don't believe Jesus is the Son of God, if you follow His teachings and live the way He instructed throughout the Gospels, you will live a better life."[24] That statement is powerful because it's rooted in truth. Jesus's teachings are a guide to living with peace, joy, and purpose, whether you approach them through faith or curiosity.

Jesus was a master at showing people how to live in alignment with love, humility, and forgiveness. His wisdom wasn't reserved for the religious or the righteous. It was for anyone willing to listen. Even his critics couldn't deny the impact of his words. He spoke to the broken, the doubters, and the outcasts, offering a way of life that could heal hearts and transform relationships.

What's often overlooked is that Jesus's message wasn't only about eternity. It was about how to live fully in the present. His teachings challenge us to release anger, envy, and selfishness, and instead embrace a life of meaning and connection. Those principles aren't abstract; they're practical steps toward a life that feels whole and fulfilling.

This chapter is an invitation to explore how aligning with those teachings can create a shift in your life. Whether you're here as a believer or someone seeking wisdom, there's something transformative about living in alignment with truth. It's like repairing broken links—each restored link strengthens the connection to your purpose, your faith, and the life you were created to live.

Jesus challenged the way we naturally view justice, inviting his followers to live in a way that defied worldly habits and expectations. The idea of willingly going beyond what's required feels unnatural, especially for someone who might be an oppressor. But that's the point. Jesus wasn't interested in fitting into what felt natural. He flipped the script to prove what's possible when we align our actions with God's heart.

Jesus's radical teachings challenge us to rise above in a world where revenge and self-preservation are often the default. He told his disciples:

> If anyone slaps you on the right cheek, turn to them the other cheek also. And if anyone wants to sue you and take your shirt, hand over your coat as well. If anyone forces you to go one mile, go with them two miles. Give to the one who asks you, and do not turn away from the one who wants to borrow from you. (Matthew 5:39–42)

Jesus echoes this same calling for active transformation later in the same passage: "Love your enemies and pray for those who persecute you" (Matthew 5:44). Think about how counterintuitive that feels. The natural reaction to someone who wrongs us is to protect ourselves, to fight back, or at the very least avoid them.

But Jesus calls us to something higher, reminding us of the impartiality of God's mercy, saying, "He causes his sun to rise on the evil and the good, and sends rain on the righteous and the unrighteous" (Matthew 5:45). God doesn't withhold His blessings based on merit, so Jesus challenges us to reflect that same kind of unconditional love.

The shock of those teachings, however, isn't actually because they are unreasonable. What's truly wild is how our world has normalized hate, selfishness, and division. Jesus's words only *feel* radical because they expose how far we've drifted from what's right. Loving those who love us back isn't extraordinary; it's expected.

Even the tax collectors, who were seen as traitors, could manage that. The real challenge is to love when it's hard, to give when it's undeserved, and to pray for those who have inflicted pain. This is the kind of love that transforms both the giver and the receiver. It is one that mends what's broken, reinforces our connection to God, and empowers us to reflect His grace in the world.

God's love doesn't operate on human terms. It is defined by the strength to rise above pride, resentment, and fear. It's unfamiliar. Loving those who harm us feels unnatural because the world often equates love with approval or agreement. But Jesus points to a higher standard, rooted in grace. The challenge here is to step into a way that feels unfamiliar and examine whether our actions reflect the love we receive freely from the Lord.

Love isn't about tolerating injustice or excusing evil. It's about breaking the cycle of resentment and repairing the chains of respect. When we open our eyes to this truth, we can see that Jesus's teachings aren't crazy. They are the cure for a world that's lost its way. And the question we have to ask ourselves is this: *Are we willing to embrace that kind of love, even when it feels impossible?* If we can't accept it within, we'll never have the strength or authenticity to extend it outward.

Renew Your Mind

Do not be anxious about anything,
but in every situation, by prayer
and petition, with thanksgiving,
present your requests to God. And the
peace of God, which transcends all

understanding, will guard your hearts
and your minds in Christ Jesus.
(Philippians 4:6–7)

Have you ever felt like your thoughts are running the show, dragging you in directions you never wanted to go? That's the battle we face every day—the battle for our minds. But the often overlooked truth is that you don't have to stay stuck in that cycle. God has given us the tools to renew our minds and live with peace, passion, and purpose.

Paul's powerful reminder in Philippians 4 describes God's authentic, active peace. It's a force that stands guard over your thoughts and emotions when you surrender them to Him. But here's the key: It also requires action on our part.

God *forgives* our sins at salvation, but He also gives us the power to *overcome* sin and renew our minds daily. This gift requires diligent work and development. It's like going to the gym. You don't build muscle by working out once; you build it through consistent time, energy, and effort. Renewing your mind and spirit works the same way. It's a daily commitment to study the Word, surrender to Jesus, and allow the Holy Spirit to guide each step you take.

Pastor Tim Timberlake, while guest preaching at VOUS Church in Miami, said something that hits home: "Even though we live on earth, we're citizens of heaven."[25] He reminds us that we're *working* here on earth, but our true home is with God. And because of that, we *can*, we *will*, and we *must* follow Jesus through the power of the Holy Spirit. That's not a suggestion; it's a call to action.

But we have to be honest with ourselves. Renewing our mind is a battle. Every day we're bombarded with messages, temptations, and seemingly harmless distractions that pull us away from God's truth. That's why we must continue analyzing our perspective and mindset daily. *Are my thoughts, behaviors, and attitude aligned with God's vision? Am I allowing the world to dictate my direction?* These aren't easy questions to ask, but they are necessary to answer.

One way to keep yourself in check is to consistently audit your attention. *Who and what is my energy poured into? Is it God's truth, or is it the endless scroll of social media, entertainment that leaves me spiraling, or the negativity of the daily headlines?*

The answer to understanding our minds is simple: GIGO— Garbage In, Garbage Out. If you're constantly feeding your mind toxicity, it's going to show up in your life. It'll lead to stress, anxiety, and even physical ailments such as heart issues, nausea, or headaches. But when you fill your mind with God's Word, you create a safe space for clarity, peace, and purpose to prosper.

Paul offers a powerful thought filter in Philippians 4:8 : "Finally, brothers and sisters, whatever is true, whatever is noble, whatever is right, whatever is pure, whatever is lovely, whatever is admirable—if anything is excellent or praiseworthy—think about such things."

This isn't just a nice idea to cling to when things get tough; it's a road map for renewing your mind in every stage of life. Each step of revival repairs the broken links that hold you back, freeing you from the weight of old limitations and unlocking the clarity to step boldly into your purpose. Filter your thoughts daily. If they don't align with God's truth and your mission, they don't belong in your mind.

Ultimately, you decide what to focus on. While you can't control every thought that pops into your head, you have the power to determine which ones stay. Feed your inner hero, not your inner villain. Be a thermostat set to the temperature based on God's truth rather than a thermometer that reacts to the shifting world around you. Renewing your mind is a daily practice, and committing to it uncovers a peace that truly transcends understanding.

Our reactions to life's challenges serve as a spotlight on our faith, revealing what's really going on around us and within us. As the Bible tells us, God willingly chose to adopt us and takes great pride in calling us His children. That's a powerful truth. The Creator of the universe calls *you* His own. Being part of God's family means we're called to act and react differently, especially when life throws curveballs.

Everything was perfect before sin entered the world. God designed us to live within His perfect Kingdom forever. But too often we act like spoiled little kids doing things our way instead of the Lord's way. Our reactions are one of the clearest ways people see whether we're living for Jesus or just saying we are. *Do I respond to challenges like the world, or do I respond like Jesus taught us?*

Gandhi once said, "If it weren't for Christians, I'd be a Christian."[26] That stings, doesn't it? He wasn't rejecting Christ; he was pointing out how often Christians fail to reflect Jesus's teachings. And one of the biggest areas we fall short in is how we respond to life's circumstances.

Too often we respond like the world does: quick to anger, defensiveness, or even hate. Someone cuts us off in traffic, and we lay on the horn. Someone wrongs us, and we hold a grudge. Someone embarrasses us, and we retaliate. These knee-jerk reactions are the *default mode* of our human nature. But as followers of Jesus, we're called to something radically different.

Pastor Andy Stanley labels this shift as "Over and Under Reactions."[27] It's about responding in a way that astounds people, stopping them in their tracks to wonder, "What's different about them?" Rather than responding with anger, God calls us to tap into patience, grace, and love. So when someone cuts you off in traffic, slow down and give them more room. When someone wrongs you, pray for them. When someone tries to embarrass you, offer the kindness they are clearly missing. These are the practices Jesus modeled in his life as a Savior and a friend.

We can't be naive to the difficulty of this change, contradicting everything our instincts suggest. That's why we can't do it alone. Only the Holy Spirit can empower us to react like Jesus, but only when we seek his help and put it into practice.

Remember, it takes practice. Start small. Begin at home with the people closest to you. When your loved ones do something that bothers you, embrace the opportunity to practice "Over and Under Reacting" in real time. Respond with love and compassion, even when it's hardest. Not only will this start to change how you feel about the situation, but it might even inspire them to meet you halfway, transforming your reactions and relationships.

The Bible reminds us, "As surely as I am the living God, says the Lord, everyone will kneel before me, and everyone will confess that I am God" (Romans 14:11 GNT). One day, every knee will bow, and every tongue will confess. Until that day, our reactions are one of the most powerful ways we can point people to Jesus. So let's commit to living out this truth—not perfectly, but intentionally. Let's astound the world with how we react and in doing so point them to the One who transforms hearts and renews minds.

Faith in Action

For it is by grace you have been saved,
through faith—and this is not from
yourselves, it is the gift of God—not
by works, so that no one can boast.
(Ephesians 2:8–9)

We are saved by grace through faith, not by anything we've done or could ever do. Salvation is a gift from God, freely given through His Son, Jesus Christ. It's not something we can earn, and it's not something we can achieve through our own efforts.

The parable of the bags of gold in Matthew 25:14–30 reminds us that God entrusts each of us with unique gifts—our time, talents, and resources. In the story, the master gives his servants different amounts of gold, each according to their ability, and expects them to use it wisely. This isn't about how much you've been given; it's about what you do with it.

The servants who invested and multiplied their gold were praised, while the one who buried his gold out of fear was rebuked. This illustrates a key truth: God calls us to be faithful stewards, using what He's given us to serve others and glorify Him. Jesus explains, "For whoever has will be given more, and they will have an abundance. Whoever does not have, even what they have will be taken from them" (Matthew 25:29).

Pride and ego can distort this perspective. They make us think that what we have is ours alone, that we've earned it, or that it's meant solely for our benefit. But the parable reminds us that everything we have is on loan from God. When we let pride take over, we risk burying our gifts—whether out of fear, selfishness, or a desire to protect our own image. The servant who buried his gold didn't just waste an opportunity; he failed to trust the master's purpose.

Think about how often we let our egos dictate our reactions. When something doesn't go according to plan, pride steps in, and suddenly our emotions take control. A single circumstance can spiral into frustration, anger, or even despair, all because we've allowed our pride to influence our perspective.

So how do we stop this chain reaction? How do we repair the connection to God that pride so often breaks? The answer is simple: Focus on Jesus. When we fix our eyes on him, pride loses its grip. Seek the Holy Spirit's guidance and immerse yourself in Jesus's teachings. Remember that everything we have—our time, our talents, our resources—is on loan from God. We are stewards, entrusted with these gifts to use them wisely and for His glory.

Jesus will hold you up and keep you safe until the day you stand before God in heaven. And on that day, God will ask each of us what we did with the gifts He gave us. Did we use our time, talents, and treasures to serve ourselves, or did we use them to serve others and further His Kingdom?

So ask yourself today: *Am I multiplying the gifts God has entrusted to me, or am I holding them back?* Pride tells us to focus on ourselves, but humility reminds us that everything we have is a gift from God. When we live as stewards, not owners, we align our hearts with His purpose. And when we do that, we strengthen our connection to Him and live the life we were created for.

God calls us to turn good intentions into meaningful actions, trusting Him to multiply our efforts. It's not enough to simply think, believe, or feel what's right; God calls us to act, behave, and do what's righteous. Many people fall into the trap of believing that good intentions alone are pleasing to God, but the Bible, especially in James, makes it clear that it's our actions—rooted in His Word—that truly matter. God loves our initiative, not just our intentions. While others may focus on the heart behind our actions, what truly inspires and influences those around us is how we turn those intentions into tangible steps.

Think about the story in John 6:1–14 where Jesus feeds the 5,000. The disciples, overwhelmed by the crowd's needs, told Jesus they didn't have enough resources to feed everyone. But Jesus asked, "What do you have with you now?"

A young boy stepped forward with five barley loaves and two small fish—essentially a handful of crackers and sardines. With childlike faith, he offered what little he had, and Jesus used it to perform a miracle, feeding many more than 5,000 people when women and children were counted. The lesson here? Limitations aren't about what we don't have but what little we have and don't use.

This same principle is echoed in Exodus 4:2 when God asked Moses, "What is that in your hand?" Moses held a simple shepherd's staff, but God used it to perform miracles, provide for millions, and even part the Red Sea. What Moses saw as an ordinary tool God used to accomplish extraordinary things. The message is clear: God will never ask us to do something we're not already equipped to handle. He uses the skills, talents, and resources we already have to fulfill His purpose.

At the end of our lives, we'll stand before God and answer two questions: *What did you do with my Son, Jesus? What did you do with the gifts I gave you?* God has entrusted each of us with unique abilities—our eyes, ears, body, heart, brain, speech, and more. Some are given additional resources or opportunities, but all of us are called to be good stewards of what we've been given. Did we use our blessings to help others, or did we hoard them for ourselves? Did we lift up the less fortunate, or did we take advantage of them?

Rick Warren's *The Purpose Driven Life* outlines five key purposes for why we're here:

- To know and love God (worship)
- To grow spiritually and imitate Jesus (discipleship)
- To love others as ourselves (fellowship)
- To serve others with our time, talent, and treasure (ministry)
- To share our life message about Jesus and what God has done for us (witness)[28]

These purposes remind us that our lives are not about accumulation or self-preservation; they're about living for God, serving others, and sharing His love. Faith in action means offering what we have back to God and trusting Him to do the rest. It's about stepping out in obedience, even when we don't see the full picture.

Like the boy with his lunch or Moses with his staff, we're called to trust God with everything in our lives, knowing that He can take what seems small and insignificant and use it for His glory. Let's stop putting limits on what God can do through us and start living with bold, childlike faith.

Rationalizing pulls us away from the truth. When we rationalize, we rationalize lies. It's the story we tell ourselves to justify staying in the same place, avoiding the discomfort of change. But faith calls us to something deeper—a healing of the heart and mind. The Bible uses the word *repent*, which in its original Greek form, *metanoia*, means a complete renewal—a rebuilding of the mind, a healing of the heart. This isn't about regret or guilt; it's about stepping into the person God created you to be with the Holy Spirit guiding you every step of the way.

Many people spend their lives fighting to get back to where they started, but God doesn't want to take you back. He wants to create something new. Our lives are broken because of sin, but God doesn't only erase the brokenness; He *uses* it. He wants us to turn away from living for ourselves and align our lives with Him. That's where true transformation begins.

Free will plays a big role here. God didn't create robots. He gave us the ability to choose, and sometimes those choices lead to pain—for ourselves and for others. When someone drinks and drives, causing devastation, that's not God's will. That's the consequence of free will. But even in the midst of our worst decisions, God's faithfulness remains. Jesus said, "I give them eternal life, and they will never perish. No one can snatch them away from me" (John 10:28 NLT). That's the promise we hold onto. No matter how far we fall, His love never lets go.

So how do we move forward?

- **Recognize Your Need for God**

  The first step is admitting that we can't do this on our own. Understanding God's nature—His love, His grace, His desire for us to live a purposeful life—is the foundation.

- **Repent and Seek Forgiveness**

  Repentance is more than feeling sorry; it's a complete shift in how we think and live. Confess your sins to Jesus and ask for His forgiveness. He's the only one who can repair the broken connection between you and God.

- **Focus on the Weak Links**

  Identify the areas in your life where the links are weakest—whether it's addiction, anger, pride, or something else. Focus your energy on what God says about those areas and turn to Jesus for help.

- **Take Action Toward Healing**

  Healing isn't just between you and God; it's also about the people around you. If your actions have hurt others, seek their forgiveness. Confess your transgressions and allow the healing process to ripple outward.

- **Trust in the Promise of Salvation**

  Once you're born again, you cannot be "unborn." Jesus promised to keep you safe until you reach heaven. Even when life feels overwhelming, hold onto that assurance.

God's plan for you is about progress over perfection. *It's about turning your pain into purpose, your mess into your message.* And here's the most important thing: You don't have to do it alone. Jesus, through the power of the Holy Spirit, is ready to hold you up, strengthen your weak links, and guide you toward the life you were meant to live.

This is your moment to realign your heart, mind, and actions with God. The journey won't always be easy, but it will be worth it. Each step you take restores your connection to the Lord, link by link, until His strength flows through every aspect of your existence. Because once you're saved, you're saved for eternity. And that's a promise you can build your life on.

Eternal Perspective

*But if you look closely into the perfect law
that sets people free, and keep on paying
attention to it and do not simply listen and
then forget it, but put it into practice—you
will be blessed by God in what you do.
(James 1:25 GNT)*

Life is like a mosaic—crafted with tile, glass, and stone. If you stand just an inch away, all you see are the fragmented pieces.

Some are sharp, some are dull, some are cracked. It's easy to get caught up in the imperfections and lose sight of the bigger picture. But when you take a step back, you begin to see the Creator's design. Every piece, every color, and every crack has a distinct purpose. The same is true for your life. The struggles, the triumphs, and the mundane are all part of a greater story that God is weaving together.

This is precisely where eternal perspective comes into play. So often we focus our minds and efforts on the small, trivial situations of today, things that won't matter in five years or even five minutes. But we begin to see life differently when we shift our gaze to Jesus. The things that once consumed us lose their power. We're reminded that our purpose isn't tied to temporary circumstances but to God's eternal plan.

The Bible highlights this truth: "If you listen to the word, but do not put it into practice, you are like people who look in a mirror and see themselves as they are. They take a good look at themselves and then go away and at once forget what they look like" (James 1:23–24 GNT). These verses challenge us to live out our faith rather than simply hearing it. It's about stepping back from the mirror, the distractions of daily life, and focusing on what truly matters: God's Word and purpose for us.

We find peace by trusting the Creator of the mosaic, even in the midst of the chaos. We may not understand why certain things happen, but we can rest in the knowledge that God is working all things together for good. So ask yourself, *Is what I'm facing today shaping my eternity?* If not, it might be time to let it go. Fix your eyes on Jesus, and trust that he's crafting a beautiful sculpture from the broken pieces.

God deeply desires for all of us to join His family, and yet He gives us the freedom to choose. That's the beauty and the weight of free will. God's patience is a blessing, but it isn't endless. The time will come when Jesus returns, and when that happens, it will be instantaneous and undeniable.

Jesus entered the world as a baby, initiating the slow and deliberate process that unfolded over thirty years.[29] He came to teach us, save us, and lay the foundation of our faith. But the next time He comes will be supernatural beyond anything we can comprehend. The Bible tells us the skies will open, stars will fall, and every soul will see him. There will be no doubting or denying his power. And by then, the time to choose will have passed.

That is why the choice we make now is so critical. We're faced with decisions that require faith every day. We trust that we won't choke when eating alone, that our car will get us safely to the destination, or that the doctor will wake us up after the right surgery.

Even atheists operate on faith, though they might not realize it or admit it. A quarter of the global population identifies as nonreligious, while 9 percent consider themselves atheists.[30] When I think about that, I'm amazed by the level of faith it takes to hold onto such a belief. Nonbelievers wager their lives on the view that this life is all there is. That's a gamble I can't imagine taking.

For me, I'd rather wager the other way. I place my faith in the overwhelming evidence for Jesus—the miracles, the resurrection, and the teachings that have transformed billions of lives. I'd rather trust in the one who gave his life for me and rose again to offer eternal life. I'm not living to *avoid* judgment but to *embrace* the greatest gift ever offered.

When Jesus returns, we will stand behind him. And the amazing part? We get to choose how He stands before us, as our judge or as our Savior. But that choice has to be made now. Once He comes back, there won't be time to reconsider. Whether you believe it or not, the fact remains: We will all stand before Him in the end.

I know I'm a sinner, and I know I need a Savior. That's why I chose Jesus. I chose grace. And I want my children, my family, and everyone I love to make that same choice because at the end of the day, we have the choice between temporary satisfaction or eternal freedom. And that's a choice I'm willing to stake eternity on.

Surrendering Control

When you come looking for me,
you'll find me. Yes, when you get
serious about finding me and want
it more than anything else, I'll make
sure you won't be disappointed.
(Jeremiah 29:13 MSG)

Let's be real. Giving up control is one of the hardest things to do. We're wired to want to manage, fix, and direct every aspect of our lives. But real change, the kind that alters your heart, your mind, and your soul, only happens when you surrender. As the Bible tells us, "We all show the Lord's glory, and we are being changed to be like him. This change in us brings ever greater glory, which comes from the Lord, who is the Spirit" (2 Corinthians 3:18 NCV). God is working on us every single day, shaping us into His image. But it starts with one thing: repentance.

Repentance is a full-on change of heart. It's admitting that you've fallen short of God's purpose for you and that you can't do this life on your own. The first step is swallowing your pride and admitting you need God's help, love, mercy, and salvation.

Surrendering isn't a passive excuse to say, "Okay, God, take over." It's an intentional action to open your heart, mind, and soul to Him. It's about living with purpose, knowing that the Creator of the universe is dwelling inside you. That takes courage, humility, and a willingness to let go of the world's lies. The world tells us we're not enough—that we need to work harder, look better, or be smarter. But God's truth is the opposite. Paul reminds us, "Don't you realize that your body is the temple of the Holy Spirit, who lives in you and was given to you by God? You do not belong to yourself" (1 Corinthians 6:19 NLT).

When you truly live with the knowledge that Jesus is walking with you through every situation, it changes everything. The pain, suffering, and heartbreak are still there, but you're not alone in it. Jesus feels it with you at a magnitude we can't even comprehend.

Think about the comfort of having a close friend or family member sit with you in your pain. Now multiply that by infinity. That's what Jesus offers. He's the ultimate comforter, the one who loves you more deeply than anyone on earth ever could. Jesus stands by, waiting patiently for you to invite Him in. Seeking Him first opens the door to true change. That's the key: seeking Him with everything you've got.

So what does that look like in real life? Start your day with prayer, dive into God's Word, and make time to connect with Him, even when life gets busy. Let go of the need to control every outcome and trust that God's plan is better than anything you could do alone. Live with the peace that comes from knowing Jesus is with you in every moment, every decision, and every challenge.

Pain has a way of stripping away the illusion of control, leaving us face to face with our own limitations. As Paul tells us, it is in moments of brokenness that God's grace becomes most evident (2 Corinthians 12:9). Surrendering to Him isn't a sign of weakness but the start of strength.

Jesus has already conquered the world, and His love is unshakable. Trusting Him doesn't mean life will be free of challenges, but it does mean we're never alone in facing them. Pain often serves as a refining fire, breaking away what doesn't serve us and revealing the strength and purpose God has placed within us.

The angels, who have never sinned, marvel at the Gospel because they've never experienced grace. No other part of creation—whether animals, plants, or nature—needs forgiveness or salvation. That's a privilege unique to humanity. Every trial, every failure, every moment of suffering is an opportunity to experience God's love in a way that's deeply personal and transformative. It's through these experiences that His glory and power are revealed.

The Bible paints a beautiful picture of God's invitation: "Listen! I am standing and knocking at your door. If you hear my voice and open the door, I will come in and we will eat together"

(Revelation 3:20 CEV). God doesn't force His way into our lives. He waits patiently, offering us the chance to invite Him in. When we do, He shares life with us, walking alongside us in every joy and every sorrow.

Pain isn't the end of the story. It's a chapter that leads to healing, growth, and a deeper understanding of God's grace. When we open the door to Him, we find not just comfort but transformation. That's the power of His love, and it's available to us every single day. The chains that once bound us weaken with every step of faith, replaced by stronger links forged in God's grace and truth. These revived links anchor us to His purpose and set us free to live truly and fully in His everlasting love.

Conclusion
How to Get to Heaven

My sheep listen to my voice; I know them, and they

follow me. I give them eternal life, and they shall

never die. No one can snatch them away from me.

(John 10:27–28 GNT)

Only the Creator can lay claim to His creation. Only the Maker can put His mark on what He made and say, "This is mine." And that's exactly what God says about you. You are His masterpiece, created with intention, love, and a purpose that only you can fulfill.

I get it. Maybe this way of thinking about your relationship with God feels a little different. Maybe you've always thought of faith as a set of rules to follow or a checklist of things to do to earn God's love. Or maybe you've been carrying guilt, pride, or shame for so long that the idea of surrendering it all to Jesus feels uncomfortable, even impossible. But the truth is that different isn't bad. In fact, different might just be exactly what you need.

What if this shift in perspective—the idea of fully submitting your life to Jesus out of trust rather than obligation—could be the key to breaking free from the rusty chains that hold you back? What if leaning into this new way of thinking could unlock the life God designed for you?

Surrendering every part of yourself to Jesus isn't about being perfect; it's about being willing. And through that willingness you can experience a connection with your Creator that's as deep and fulfilling as humanly possible while you're here on earth.

As we near the conclusion of our journey together, I pray this book has been more than just words on a page. I hope it's been a source of encouragement filled with loving advice to help you reflect on your connection to God.

Some people get overwhelmed by reading the Bible. After all, it's nearly 800,000 words, about 1,500 pages, and written over a 1,500-year span by forty authors across sixty-six books. It can appear daunting, but please know that the entire Bible is God's love story for His children. When you strip away all the debates, doctrines, and distractions, two simple truths remain: Love God and love people.

That's it.

That's the foundation of everything.

And yet it's often the simplest truths that are the hardest to live out.

I didn't dive deeply into theology or doctrine here because I believe it's best to leave that to the experts. But what I do know is that God didn't call us to argue over who's right or which church is more righteous. He called us to love. And when we make God the center of our lives, when everything we do revolves around eternity, our connection with Him becomes what it was always meant to be.

If God is your Father and God is my Father, that makes us brothers and sisters. And yet how often do we allow bitterness, judgment, and resentment to creep in and divide us? Jesus didn't tell us to *like* our neighbor; He told us to *love* them. That's a huge difference. Loving someone doesn't mean you approve of their actions or behavior. It means you care about their soul and pray for them, even when it's hard.

Take the story of the prodigal son, for example. We've all been the father, the prodigal, or the disapproving brother at different points in our life. Maybe you've been the one to wander off, chasing fleeting pleasures over eternal fulfillment. Or perhaps you've been the one standing on the sidelines, arms crossed, judging someone else's shortcomings. But the goal, or really the *challenge*, is to be like the father—to run toward others with open arms, bursting with love and compassion that others may not even deserve.

Our works do not save us. But if we truly love Jesus and want to get into heaven, our actions will innately reflect that love. It's not enough to say we follow Him on Sunday if we are living for ourselves the rest of the week. Faith without action is dead. And the world is watching. Your family, friends, and community notice how you respond when life gets hard. It's easy to praise God when things are going well. But what about when they're not?

Jesus tells us clearly that the greatest commandment is to love God with all your heart, soul, mind, and strength. That means loving Him with your words, emotions, thoughts, and actions. It means treating your body as a temple, living with purpose and passion, and repairing the broken links that separate you from Him and His love.

God doesn't yell or scream to get our attention; He whispers. Think about it. When someone is close to you, they don't need to shout for you to hear them. Their voice is gentle, intimate, and clear because of the closeness you share. That's exactly how God communicates with His children. He's right there with you, speaking directly to your heart. But you might miss it if your life is too noisy and your mind is cluttered with distractions.

It's time to weed out the worries and tune into His voice. He speaks to us in so many ways—through the Bible, through nature, through the people around us, and so often through silence. But we must be willing to stop and listen.

The Bible is our road map to heaven, our GPS for living life with meaning. We are completely lost without its hope and guidance. And the stakes couldn't be any higher. Is holding onto anger, pride, anxiety, or addiction worth risking eternity? Are you willing to trade the paradise God prepared for you for fleeting pleasures on earth?

The answer is no, and the good news is that it's never too late to turn back. You always have the choice to love God with everything you have, love others when it seems impossible, and live in a way that reflects the love that remains. Because in the end, the greatest of these is love.

The Journey of Faith: Choices and Challenges

You should not be surprised at my saying, 'You must be born again.'

(John 3:7)

God's mercy, grace, and acceptance are not things we can fully comprehend, but they are gifts we are called to embrace. How does God want us to feel when someone we disapprove of is welcomed back into His house in heaven? How can God allow racism, jealousy, resentment, or bitterness into heaven? Those feelings, behavior, and attitude simply won't fly in heaven, so it shouldn't here on earth either.

Picture life as a cruise ship. We're all aboard out at sea, and the ship represents God's Kingdom on earth. It's heading toward one destination: heaven. However, we face numerous choices and challenges along the way. There's plenty to do on this cruise—gambling, partying, indulging in pleasures. It is easy to get lost in the bells, whistles, and flashing lights of the journey and forget about the destination.

At the same time, God doesn't want us locked in our cabins praying 24/7. He calls us to live *in* His kingdom, *for* His glory, and *by* His power. There is a thin line between being *in* the world and being *of* the world, and it's not something we can identify on our own. It's only possible through the power of the Holy Spirit.

Let's reflect on the routine many people fall victim to: wake up, work, make money, eat, watch TV, sleep, repeat. Maybe there is some relaxing on the weekends or even the occasional trip, but is that really living? It sounds a lot to me like just existing.

God didn't create us merely to survive but to live for Him and thrive. Chasing happiness on human terms will always feel hollow and unfulfilling. True peace, joy, and purpose come only when our connection to God is strong and aligned. That is why we were created to begin with. When we allow Him to restore our broken links through faith, repentance, and surrender, our connection to Him becomes indestructible. That's when we truly start living. It's in that alignment where every link is forged in and by His grace that we uncover the peace we were created to encounter and exude.

God gives us the choice to live with Him in heaven forever. But with that choice comes responsibility. One day we'll stand before Him and give an account of our lives. These are the two most important questions He'll ask: (1) *Did you accept My Son, Jesus, as your Lord and Savior?* (2) *How did you love and treat others with the gifts I gave you?*

God knows every thought and every action. And while we're saved by grace through faith, we're still called to action. We have free will, and that means we're responsible for our decisions. When a thought enters your mind, you can either act on it or take control of it. How? By focusing on godly things. If you're filling your mind with porn, violence, or negativity, it's going to be tough to live the life God designed for you. The easiest way to control your mind is to follow God's commands.

We're constantly battling three enemies that distract us from God's guidance.

- **Old Self** – The person we used to be before we knew Jesus. That old mindset and old habits don't just disappear overnight. They'll try to pull you back, convincing you they were "cool" or "fun." But that's a lie.

- **Flesh** – Our earthly desires. Eating, drinking, sex, fun—none of these are bad in themselves, but when they become your main focus, when they consume your thoughts, you're living by the flesh and not the Spirit.

- **Satan** – He can't read your mind, but he's a master at distraction. He'll bombard you with tasks, tempt you to live for the moment, and fill your head with half-truths and compromises.

Let me address the Christians who might criticize this message for its lack of doctrine or theological depth. First of all, I get it; I've been there. But here's my one request: Respect the underlying message. Yes, we're saved by grace through faith, but that doesn't mean we're off the hook when it comes to action.

Jesus made it clear that pursuing Him isn't a walk in the park. He said, "If anyone would come after me, let him deny himself and take up his cross and follow me" (Matthew 16:24 ESV). That is a clear call to surrender, sacrifice, and commitment. It's a powerful reminder that the path to true discipleship requires leaving comfort behind to step into a life of faith.

The same truth rings through Jesus's command for us to "be born again" (John 3:7 ESV). Spiritual rebirth is both a gift from God and a response from us. He took the first step in love by sending His Son to die for us so we could be part of His eternal family. Our role is to act in faith, believing in His promise of eternal life through salvation.

Many people are baptized or christened when they are babies—a wonderful expression of faith by the parents, family members, and friends. This ritualistic practice is something I would recommend. You're letting everyone know that your faith in God is important to you, and you plan on raising your children accordingly. However, this may be more for the parents, family, and friends than the actual child.

When my children turned twelve, we decided collectively to get baptized as a family in the ocean with other church members. My children were baptized as babies, but they felt a longing and a calling to want to be part of it. They wanted to make that decision, and we not only embraced it but fully, wholeheartedly, and actively participated in it. Since then, their faith and church life have grown exponentially. They truly feel born again and live with purpose, passion, and meaning. They are more on fire for Jesus now than before.

All my children did was make a public announcement about their faith and how they want to live. Now they are acting it out and living their lives for God's purpose and His Kingdom-building purposes. My wife and I feel a sense of rebirth as well. How could we not? I recommend all families, regardless of the parents or children's ages, to be baptized together as a family with in-laws and extended or immediate family members. Watch how the Holy Spirit will work in your family.

This experience stretches far beyond intellectual knowledge; it's a relationship. It's talking with Jesus, walking with him, thanking him, and praying with him. It's thinking less about ourselves and more about Him and others around us. Through the power of the Holy Spirit, we can accept the gift of forgiveness.

So what's your next move? Are you ready to step into the life God designed for you—to experience His Kingdom, glory, and power in ways you've never imagined? The road ahead won't be easy, but it's worth every sacrifice, challenge, and step of faith. This is your moment to rise above the noise, align your heart with His purpose, and embrace the extraordinary life waiting on the other side of surrender. You already have what it takes. Now it's time to use it.

Salvation through Grace

My sheep listen to my voice; I know them, and they follow me. I give them eternal life, and they will never die, and no one can steal them out of my hand. My Father gave my sheep to me. He is greater than all, and no person can steal my sheep out of my Father's hand.
(John 10:27–29 NCV)

Let's start with this often overlooked truth: Salvation is a gift. It's not something we earn, deserve, or achieve through our own efforts. It's the result of God's love and mercy extended to us through Jesus Christ. We are instantly saved when we accept Jesus as our Lord and Savior. There's no application, waiting period, purification process, or checklist to complete.

Jesus made this unmistakably clear when He declared to the thief on the cross, "I promise you that today you will be in Paradise with me" (Luke 23:43 GNT). The thief didn't offer a grand gesture or a perfect prayer; he simply asked to be remembered. Yet Jesus in His boundless grace didn't just remember him; He welcomed him into eternity. That's the kind of Savior we have—one who goes above and beyond, meeting us right where we are and offering us more than we could ever dream of or deserve.

God's grace is rooted in faith—recognizing that we are broken sinners in need of a Savior. When we turn to Jesus, admitting our need and asking for forgiveness, God welcomes us into His eternal family. From that moment forward, we belong to Him, and nothing can take us out of His hands.

Yes, salvation is a gift, but it's also a call to live differently— not to earn God's love but to respond to it. James reminds us that faith without works is dead. Our actions, choices, and the fruits of our lives reveal the transformation that happens when Jesus takes hold of our hearts. It's not about being perfect; it's about the direction we're heading, aligning our lives with God's purpose and reflecting His love and grace in everything we do.

For those who reject God, the question is this: *Why?* Why would someone who spent their life running from God suddenly want to spend eternity with Him? Imagine standing before God and hearing Him ask, "Why do you want to live in my house now? You rejected me your entire life. You lived for yourself, chasing temporary pleasures and fleeting satisfaction. Why now?" It's a sobering thought, isn't it?

But for believers, the story is entirely different. Once we accept Jesus, we are adopted into God's eternal family. We become His sons and daughters, and nothing can separate us from His love. Even when we feel like we've messed up beyond repair, even when we feel spiritually dead, Jesus reminds us that we are alive in Him. Our salvation is secure—not because of what we've done but because of what God has done. God's ring of love can never be broken.

Think for a moment about the magnitude of Jesus's sacrifice. He lived a perfect, sinless life. He performed miracles, healed the sick, and taught thousands. Yet He willingly endured humiliation, torture, and death on a cross because He loves us, because He wanted to bridge the gap between us and God. The most painful part of His sacrifice wasn't the physical suffering; it was the separation from God the Father. For three days, Jesus experienced a disconnection from the perfect harmony He had always known. That's a level of pain we can't even begin to comprehend.

But Jesus's resurrection changed everything. It's the cornerstone of our faith, the source of our hope, and the guarantee of our eternal freedom. Through His death and resurrection, Jesus paid the debt we could never pay. He made a way for us to be reconciled with God, to live with purpose, and to spend eternity in His presence.

If you're feeling a tug on your heart right now, don't ignore it. Take the next step. Repair your broken link to God. Admit to God that you've been living for yourself, that you've strayed from His plan, and that you need a Savior. Turn to Jesus and thank Him for His sacrifice. Ask for His forgiveness and invite Him into your life.

Here's a simple prayer to guide you:

Jesus, please forgive me for all the sins I've committed and will commit. Thank you for dying on the cross for me. Thank you for paying the debt I could never pay. Please help me live a more purposeful, fulfilled life with passion and meaning. I submit and surrender to You. In your name, Amen.

If you prayed that prayer and meant it, congratulations! You've just been born again into a new life. You've been adopted into God's eternal family, and nothing can ever remove you from His love. Now it's time to take the next step. Find a Bible-preaching church that's alive with faith, energy, and community. Surround yourself with brothers and sisters in Christ who will encourage you, challenge you, and walk alongside you on this journey. Look for a church with mixed age groups, not just your age demographic. My personal opinion is that the churches that thrive have singles, married couples, young families, empty nesters, and older, more mature folks. Then you can all learn and do life with each other.

As your faith grows, you'll start to see life through a new lens. You may find yourself drawn to different friendships, priorities, and ways of living. That's God speaking to you, guiding you toward the life He created you for. Listen to His voice, follow His lead, and trust that His plan for you is greater than anything you could imagine. With His help, you can restore and strengthen your connection to God.

This is your moment. Step into it with faith, gratitude, and confidence, knowing that you are loved, forgiven, and forever held in the hands of your Savior.

When we think about adoption, it's a powerful image of being chosen, loved, and brought into a family—not because of what we've done, but because of the love of the one adopting us. That's exactly what God has done for us through Jesus. He didn't just save us from sin; He brought us into His family as His children.

If salvation could be earned by simply being nice or having good intentions, Jesus's sacrifice would have been unnecessary. The truth is that there was no other way. Jesus endured unimaginable pain, humiliation, and separation from God the Father to make a way for us to be adopted into God's eternal family. If there had been another path, God would have revealed it.

God's adoption of us is permanent. In Roman times under Roman law, a biological child could be disowned, but an adopted child could never be disowned. That's the kind of security we have in God's family. Once He adopts us, we are His forever. The Bible reminds us that "God's Spirit joins himself to our spirits to declare that we are God's children" (Romans 8:16 GNT).

That brings up an important question: Can we ever be disowned or removed from God's family once we're in heaven? After all, Satan was kicked out of heaven. The answer lies in understanding the difference between humans and angels. Angels are supernatural beings created for specific purposes, and some chose to turn away from God, becoming wicked and rebellious. Humans, on the other hand, are born into sin and need a Savior to rescue us. Through Jesus's redeeming work on the cross, we are saved, cleansed, and adopted into God's family.

Unlike angels, we have the unique privilege of carrying the Spirit within us. That is what transforms us and secures our place in God's family. We are not only saved from sin; we are made heirs of the Creator of the universe. As adopted children, we are given a new identity, a new purpose, and a permanent place in God's family.

This adoption is not something we could ever earn or deserve; it's a gift of grace. And once we are in God's family, we are there forever. That's the beauty of being adopted by God. It's not just a relationship but a covenant, an unbreakable bond linking us to God that assures us of His love and our place in His eternal Kingdom.

The Greatest Deal Ever Offered

For God so loved the world that He
gave His only begotten Son, that
whoever believes in Him should not
perish but have everlasting life.
(John 3:16 NKJV)

My profession affords me to speak, corroborate, and advise some of the world's wealthiest individuals and families. We make deals together weekly. My career is based on deal-making. So let's make sure we fully understand this agreement. Our salvation is the greatest deal ever offered and the greatest deal that could ever exist. No matter what you've done, how far you've strayed, or how broken you feel, God offers you a fresh start. Your past, present, and future sins are *forgiven* and *forgotten* through Jesus.

And in exchange, you're adopted into God's chosen family and get eternity in paradise with him. That's not a deal; that's a miracle.

We are God's masterpiece. He loves us too much to leave us the way the world tries to mold us. He desires nothing more than for us to run back into His arms. When we align our thoughts, actions, and hearts with Jesus, we're not only preparing for eternity; we're living the best possible life on earth as well.

Living with purpose means stepping into the unique role God created for you. You don't have to be perfect; you just have to allow God to use you exactly as you are.

Every saint has a past, and every sinner has a future.

No matter how far you've fallen or how broken you feel, God can and will use you for His glory.

God doesn't need you to have it all together. In fact, He often works through our weaknesses, our hurts, and our struggles. He uses the broken parts of us. It's His power, not ours, that shines through. You have to choose to accept His call. You have to be willing to say, "Here I am, Lord. Use me."

God cares more about the *why* behind your actions than the *what*. When your motives are pure and your focus is on Him, He'll guide you every step of the way. If you feel God calling you to something bigger, keep your eyes on Him. The bigger you see God, the smaller your problems and challenges will seem. When you focus on His eternal perspective, the tasks at hand won't feel so overwhelming.

Just as an athlete works out daily to build strength and endurance, we need to develop a spiritual workout routine. That means spending time in prayer, diving into God's Word, and aligning your thoughts with His truth. You create a kind of "spiritual muscle memory" when you do that consistently. Even when life gets tough, your habits and routines will pull you back to God's perspective. For every one of life's trials and tribulations, there is a Bible verse to overcome any challenge or circumstance.

Just like an athlete needs rest and nourishment to perform at their best, we need the same balance spiritually. Most people fall hardest when they're exhausted, overwhelmed, or spiritually drained. That's why it's so important to take care of your mind, body, and soul. Rest in God's presence, stay hydrated with His Word, fuel your spirit with His promises, and strengthen the links connecting you to God.

The key to unlocking your true purpose is to stop striving and start surrendering. Allow the Lord to work through you, trusting His authority over your fears and failures. Answer the knock and invite in the light. Living for God is an investment in eternity. You can step into your purpose with confidence, guaranteed that you are called, equipped, and *never* alone.

I'm a businessman, and I've seen a lot of deals in my life. For over thirty years I've been presented with several deals a week. That's thousands of deals. But let me tell you, nothing—*nothing*—comes close to the deal God offers. It's not merit-based like so many other belief systems. It's not about earning your way or proving your worth. It's about grace, love, and accepting the gift that Jesus already paid for.

Most other religions are all about what *you* have to do. Be good enough, act a certain way, follow a set of rules, and maybe you'll earn some sort of reward. But God's deal? It's the complete opposite. It's all about what Jesus already did. He lived a perfect life, died a brutal death, and rose again to offer us eternal freedom with him.

This deal is available to *everyone*. No matter who you are, where you've been, or what you've done, all you have to do is say yes. Ask Jesus to forgive your sins, invite Him into your heart, and accept the gift of salvation. That's it. No strings attached.

Why wouldn't you take this deal? Why wouldn't you say yes to the greatest offer in history? I'm not asking out of judgment or assumption but out of a genuine desire for you to identify what is holding you captive. Whatever it is, those are the broken links that are keeping you from stepping into the life God has for you.

Maybe it's fear. Maybe it's doubt. Maybe it's the story you've told yourself for years—that you're not good enough, that you've made too many mistakes, that being religious isn't cool or fun, or that it's too late for you. Those are the lies the enemy uses to keep you from experiencing the freedom and love God is offering. Some of the greatest people I know—some of the strongest leaders, world class communicators, most successful business people, and most of the world's greatest athletes— are Christians. Anyone who knows these people personally are attracted to them. There is a magnetic force that draws you to them. You may not even know that they are purposeful practicing Christians, but something is drawing you to them.

Identify those lies. Once you do, you can hand them over to Jesus. He's the only one who can break their power over you for good. And when they fall away, you'll finally be free to step into the life you were created for—a life of purpose, joy, and eternal connection with the Creator of the universe. The chain linking you to God is forged by His love for you and your love for Him. His love for you can never be broken.

This is it. This is your moment. Don't let those lies and your sin hold you back any longer. Say yes to Jesus and watch as He takes the broken pieces of your life and turns them into something more beautiful than you could ever imagine. Step into it with faith, courage, and confidence that you are loved beyond measure.

You've got this. And more importantly, God's got you.

Acknowledgments

This book has been shaped and inspired by the wisdom, teachings, and examples of many incredible spiritual leaders. I express my deepest gratitude to:

- Rick Warren
- Rich Wilkerson Jr.
- Craig Groeschel
- Timothy Keller
- Judah Smith
- Stephen Hickson
- Chad Veach
- Joel Osteen
- Charles Stanley
- Steven Furtick
- Michael Todd
- Joyce Meyer
- Tim Timberlake

About the Author

Anthony Caravetta is a devoted husband, father, and faith author whose life's mission is to help people discover the fullness of who they were created to be. A longtime career Wall Streeter and wealth advisor by profession, Anthony has guided individuals and families through seasons of abundance and seasons of immense hardship. During these personal encounters, he observed a deep and consistent human reality: even people who sincerely believe in God and have soulful hope of eternity often struggle through life feeling disconnected, overwhelmed, or spiritually unfulfilled.

This insight inspired Anthony to step beyond the world of finance and write Broken Links, a heartfelt and accessible exploration of why so many people still feel anxious, weary, or distant from God—and how they can restore the intimacy, connection and peace He promises.

Anthony writes not as a theologian but as a fellow traveler, a man who has experienced the beauty and the breaking points of life, and who has come to know firsthand that even the world's wealthiest families still struggle emotionally, relationally and spiritually.

His writing blends biblical truth, personal reflection, and practical wisdom, offering a pathway for readers to find meaning, significance, purpose and passion in a transformative way.

Anthony lives in South Florida with his wife, Danielle, and their twins. When he is not writing or advising families, Anthony is still very active in sports, as a former collegiate football player, and is heavily involved in his church, supports leadership roles, sits on boards and invests deeply in helping people live grounded, purposeful lives.

Endnotes

1 Randy Alcorn, Heaven (Carol Stream, IL: Tyndale House Publishers, 2004), 23, referencing K. Connie Kang, "Next Stop, the Pearly Gates," Los Angeles Times, October 24, 2003, https://www.latimes.com/archives/la-xpm-2003-oct-24-na-heaven24-story.html.

2 Rick Warren, "Change the Way You Think," Pastor Rick's Daily Hope, May 21, 2025,

3 Rick Warren, "Talking to Your Heavenly Father, Seeking God for a Breakthrough — Part 4," Saddleback Church, December 4, 2016,

4 I suggest starting each morning by reading a verse from Proverbs. Most of the proverbs were written by the wisest person who ever lived: King Solomon.

5 Strong's Hebrew Concordance Online, s.v. "hesed," accessed July 28, 2025, https://biblehub.com/hebrew/2618.htm.

6 Lee Strobel, A Case for Christ: A Journalist's Personal Investigation of the Evidence for Jesus (Grand Rapids: Zondervan, 1998).

7 Aaron Baker, "What Is the Difference Between Sin, Iniquity, and Transgressions?" Seeking Scripture, accessed August 12, 2025, https://seekingscripture.com/what-is-the-difference-between-sin-iniquity-and-transgressions/.

8 Strong's Hebrew Concordance Online, s.v. "pesha," accessed August 12, 2025, https://biblehub.com/hebrew/6588.htm.

9 Strong's Hebrew Concordance Online, s.v. "avon," accessed August 12, 2025, https://biblehub.com/hebrew/5771.htm.

10 Strong's Exhaustive Concordance Online, s.v. "hupokrités," accessed August 12, 2025, https://biblehub.com/greek/5273.htm.

11 Strong's Exhaustive Concordance Online, s.v. "homologeó," accessed August 12, 2025, https://biblehub.com/greek/3670.htm.

12 Rick Warren, "Are You Telling Yourself the Truth?" Daily Hope, accessed August 21, 2025, https://www.lightsource.com/ministry/daily-hope/articles/are-you-telling-yourself-the-truth-19471.html.

13 Jonathan Van Horn, "Athlete: Take Action and Be Transformed," Athletes in Action, accessed August 21, 2025, https://athletesinaction.org/devotional/athlete-take-action-and-be-transformed/.

14 Jonathan Van Horn, "Athlete: Take Action and Be Transformed," Athletes in Action, accessed August 21, 2025, https://athletesinaction.org/devotional/athlete-take-action-and-be-transformed/.

15 Brad Komgenick, "7,000 Promises!!" God's Light Christian Counseling, April 13, 2016, https://godslightcc.wordpress.com/2016/04/13/7000-promises/.

16 Dallas Shepard, "When Neuroscience and Our Faith Intersect," Harmonized Brain Centers Blog, December 20, 2024, https://www.harmonizedbraincenters.com/post/when-neuroscience-and-our-faith-intersect.

17 Rick Warren, "How to Overcome Persistent Temptations with Rick Warren & Tom Holladay," YouTube, March 25, 2019.

18 Amy Arnsten, Carolyn M. Mazure, and Rajita Sinha, "This Is Your Brain in Meltdown," Scientific American 306, no. 4 (2012): 48–53, doi:10.1038/scientificamerican0412-48.

19 Tim Keller, Walking with God through Pain and Suffering (New York: Dutton, 2013).

20 Tim Keller, "A Transcription of Tim Keller's 'Your Plans: God's Plans,'" Reformed Evangelist, December 25, 2015.

21 Rich Wilkerson Jr. "Learning to Receive from Jesus," YouTube, May 19, 2020.

22 Got Questions Ministries, "Is the Divorce Rate Among Christians Truly the Same as Among Non-Christians?" accessed August 28, 2025.

23 Rick Warren, "Rick's Grace Story," accessed September 8, 2025, https://www.theotherrickwarren.com/story.

24 Andy Stanley, "Letting Go," North Point Community Church, accessed September 5, 2025.

25 Tim Timberlake, "I Ain't There Yet . . . The Art of Joy," VOUS Church, July 17, 2022.

26 Kevin Carson, "'If It Weren't for Christians, I'd Be a Christian' – Gandhi," KevinCarson, July 25, 2019.

27 Andy Stanley, "Reactions Speak Louder Than Words • Part 2 'Over and Under Reactions,'" Your Move with Andy Stanley, December 8, 2023.

28 Rick Warren, The Purpose Driven Life (Grand Rapids: Zondervan, 2013).

29 Rick Warren, "Next Time Will Be Different," Sermons.Love, accessed September 8, 2025.

30 WIN-Gallup International, "Global Index of Religiosity and Atheism – 2012," accessed September 9, 2025, https://web.archive.org/web/20171114113506/http://www.wingia.com/web/files/news/370/file/370.pdf.